D0408174

The Poles
in America

ETHNIC CHRONOLOGY SERIES
NUMBER 9

The Poles in America
1608-1972

A Chronology & Fact Book

Compiled and edited by

Frank Renkiewicz

1973
OCEANA PUBLICATIONS, INC.
DOBBS FERRY, NEW YORK

Library of Congress Cataloging in Publication Data

Renkiewicz, Frank, 1935-
    The Poles in America, 1608-1972.

    (Ethnic chronology series, no. 9)
    SUMMARY: Chronologically traces the history and
accomplishments of Poles in the United States from
1608-1972. Includes reproductions of documents
pertinent to Polish-American history.
    Bibliography: p.
    1. Poles in the United States--History.
1. Poles in the United States   I. Title.
II. Series.
E184.P7R46   301.45'19'185073   73-1879
ISBN 0-379-00502-6

Manufactured in the United States of America

TABLE OF CONTENTS

EDITOR'S FOREWORD

It is now more than three and one-half centuries since the people of the old Polish Commonwealth first joined other Europeans in the settlement of North America. Farmers, workers, gentlemen, soldiers and writers, they took an honorable though mostly individual part in the colonial and early national history of the United States. The origins of the Polish ethnic community in the new nation lie rather in the aftermath of the Polish insurrection against Russia in 1830-1831, one of many efforts to undo the partition of Poland by its neighbors. Hundreds of exiles, most of them middle class and gentry socially, came to the United States in the age of Jackson, established new lives for themselves, but continued to think of themselves as Polish and founded the first Polish institutions in their adopted country. Meanwhile, fundamental changes in the agriculture of Poland, particularly its commercialization, led to the migration of thousands of peasants to the farmlands and industrial centers of Texas, the Great Lakes States and the Northeast after 1854.

As their number grew rapidly in the 1870's, the new and mostly urban immigrants organized the basic institutions -- mutual aid and fraternal societies, national parishes, parochial schools, building and loan associations, neighborhood-oriented businesses and political clubs -- which still sustain the ethnic community. Their leaders, the Roman Catholic clergy, professional people with a secular and liberal orientation, American-bred community leaders, struggled meanwhile to unify and define the immigration according to their respective lights. Stalemated in their efforts to mold Polish America within a single ideology, the leaders turned after 1890 to securing a measure of local religious and political autonomy for the ethnic communities. Their campaign for self-determination reached a kind of grand climax in the successful fight for the independence of Poland itself in World War I.

The growth of a native-born generation of Polish Americans between 1900 and 1940 raised the long-term question of assimilation to American life. Men and women who spoke English as a native language, who were educated in the values of Anglo-American culture and who were sometimes successful in making their way in the larger society gradually became the majority. As late as the 1960's, however, Polish Americans still clustered in large communities often not far removed from the first neighborhoods of the late nineteenth century, tended to resemble other working class groups with recent immigrant backgrounds and retained a sense of their Polish identity while seeking a measure of national recognition and leadership.

The chronology which follows marks the major events in the evolution of the Polish American community; the documents, mostly in the words of Polish Americans themselves, comment on their experience in the New World. Whatever is good there rests, as all surveys must, upon the work of hundreds of researchers in the history of Polish America. The faults and errors are mine alone.

Frank Renkiewicz
College of St. Teresa
Winona, Minnesota

CHRONOLOGY

1608 The ship Mary and Margaret arrived in Jamestown, Virginia, carrying at least two Poles, probably to serve as makers of pitch, tar and soap ashes for export. They soon earned reputations as reliable workmen and assisted John Smith, the president of the colony's council, in combat with the Indians. They were the first Poles to settle in the New World; several others followed in the early years of the colony.

1619 Polish settlers in Virginia demanded--and received--the franchise in the colony in the same year as the convening of the House of Burgesses and the beginning of representative government in the New World.

1643 Isaac Jogues, the French Jesuit missionary, recorded the first clear instance of Polish settlement in New Amsterdam (later New York City).

1662 Albert Saborishki (Zaborowski) arrived in New Amsterdam. Possibly from Prussia, he was Lutheran in religion and at least partly Polish in ancestry. He became the progenitor of the numerous and distinguished Zabriskie clan of New Jersey. During its first century in America, the Zabriskie family was assimilated to Dutch and then to Anglo-American culture.

1730 Anthony Sadowski of Pennsylvania and later of Virginia was active as a pioneer trader in the Ohio Valley-Great Lakes region at about this time. His sons participated in the exploration and settlement of the Ohio Valley later in the eighteenth century.

1750 Poles may have been among the Moravian Brethren who settled in Pennsylvania in the third quarter of the eighteenth century.

1776 Tadeusz Kosciuszko reached Philadelphia from France in August and was commissioned a Colonel in the Engineers of the Continental Army. His first assignment was in constructing the defenses of Philadelphia and the Delaware River.

1777
Kosciuszko took a major role in planning fortifications in northern New York where his designs and advice on the choice of battlefields helped the Americans defeat the English at Saratoga in October.

Kazimierz Pulaski arrived in Boston from France in July to join in the War of American Independence. Earlier, in Poland, he had participated in the Confederation of Bar, an unsuccessful movement of the Polish gentry to weaken the influence of Russia and reforming noblemen in their country. He saw action at the battle of Brandywine Creek in September and advised the Americans on the formation of their cavalry in 1777-1778.

1778
Kosciuszko supervised the building of the defenses of West Point, the key to the Hudson River Valley, in 1778-1780.

1779
Pulaski was mortally wounded at the siege of Savannah in October.

1781
Kosciuszko commanded transportation during General Nathaniel Greene's successful defensive campaign against the English army of Lord Cornwallis in the Carolinas.

1783
Kosciuszko helped to found the Society of the Cincinnati, the major Revolutionary War veterans organization, and was promoted to the rank of Brigadier-General. He returned to France in the following year.

The number of Polish participants in the War for Independence is uncertain. Miecislaus Haiman estimated that twelve Poles may have served as officers and that about one hundred Americans of Polish descent were members of the opposing armies.

1795
Poland was partitioned for the third time by Austria, Prussia and Russia and disappeared as an independent state until 1918. The three sections followed somewhat different paths politically and economically, but Polish nationalism and the sense of Poland's cultural unity grew stronger in the nineteenth century.

1797
Kosciuszko returned to the United States following his release from imprisonment in Russia for leading the Polish insurrection of 1794. The visit allowed him to go to France the next year where he was a link between the Republican party leader Thomas Jefferson and the leaders of Revolutionary France.

Julian Ursyn Niemcewicz--author, reformer, aide-de-camp to Kosciuszko to 1794--accompanied his former commander and fellow prisoner to America. He spent most of the next decade in the United States, traveling widely and recording his impressions of the country in several literary works.

1821   Father Francis Dzierozynski arrived in the United States following the expulsion of the Jesuits, of whom he was one, from Russia. His mission was to reorganize and direct the American Jesuit community. As provincial of the Maryland province of this Catholic religious order in the 1840's he helped to found the College of the Holy Cross in Worcester, Massachusetts.

1830   A major rebellion against Russian rule broke out in Poland. Its failure in the next year led to the "Great Emigration" and the growth of a large Polish community in exile.

1834   234 Poles, exiles after the uprising in 1830-1831, arrived in New York harbor from Austria on March 28. While still aboard ship they formed the Polish Committee in America, the first Polish organization in America, to speak for them to the American authorities. Their number grew to about 425 in the next two years. American public opinion was strongly sympathetic to their problems.

The United States Congress responded to the appeal of the Polish exiles for land on which to build a "Little Poland" with a land grant in Illinois. However, this project was abandonned by 1842.

1842   Paul Sobolewski and Eustace Wyszynski published several issues of Poland-Historical, Literary, Monumental and Picturesque in New York under the auspices of a Polish Literary Society in America. Printed in English, it attempted to inform Americans about the history of Poland. Though it may have been a book printed in parts, it might also qualify as the first Polish periodical publication in the United States.

1846   Fresh disturbances broke out in Poland, this time in the portion occupied by Austria. The most prominent exile to America from this uprising was John Tyssowski, the so-called "Dictator of Cracow," who later received several federal appointments.

Major Gaspard Tochman, an exile of the revolution of 1830-1831, organized the Polish Slavonian Literary Association in New York City. Its members were prominent native and Polish Americans. Its inspiration was, in Tochman's words: "That a Slavonian should desire that the glory of his sires should be known abroad; that he should desire that the reminiscences of his race keep alive abroad a sympathy, and add the weight of the moral power to the scale of its destiny; this seems to be just and natural."

1849

Dr. Felix Paul Wierzbicki, pioneer in the Far West, published California As It Is in San Francisco. It was an important contemporary account of California in the Gold Rush Days and the first English-language book published west of the Rocky Mountains. Wierzbicki later helped to organize the first medical society in San Francisco.

1852

Cyprian Norwid, a major Polish romantic poet, arrived in New York City for a stay of two years in the United States.

The Democratic Society of Polish Emigres in America was founded in New York City and remained active until 1858. Affiliated with the more radical wing of the Polish exile community, it leaned toward the new Republican party and condemned slavery in the United States.

1854

Kalikst Wolski, a Polish engineer, visited the North American Phalanx in New Jersey. This colony was based on the principles of the French Socialist Francois Fourier who favored the creation of associations just large enough to meet all social and industrial needs. Soon afterwards, Wolski helped to found the unsuccessful phalanx of La Reunion in Texas.

A contingent of Silesian Polish peasants left for America in September, reaching Galveston, Texas early in December and what became Panna Maria in Texas on December 24. Traditionally, they represent the beginning of the mass, peasant, "economic" migration to the United States. This first Polish colony in America was strengthened by new arrivals in 1855-1856. Father Leopold Moczygenba served as its first pastor and unofficial leader.

1860

The sculptor Henry Dmochowski-Sanders returned to Poland after a long and successful career in the United States. His busts of Pulaski and Kosciuszko, which stand in the Capitol in Washington, are the most famous of his many commissions.

Gaspard Tochman, now a resident of Virginia, supported Stephen Douglas for the presidency and was elected a member of the Electoral College.

1861

After the election of Lincoln, Tochman joined those who tried to mediate between the North and the South and to avoid war. After Lincoln's proclamation of a state of rebellion and call to arms, he supported the Confederate cause and initiated the formation of a unit called the "Polish Brigade" in Louisiana. The brigade consisted mostly of Irish, French, Germans and a few native Americans.

Adam Gurowski, an erratic exile in America since 1849, was appointed to a minor post in the State Department. As an ally of radical Republican politicians (like Charles Sumner) in Congress, he worked for more vigorous prosecution of the war against the Confederacy and to undermine the position of conservative Republicans. He was dismissed from the Department for publication of his Diary, a critical inside view of the Administration, in 1862.

During the summer Wlodzimierz Krzyzanowski organized the 58th New York Infantry. Later known as the "Polish Legion," it was composed of Germans, Poles, Danes, Frenchmen, Italians, Russians and Hungarians.

1862

Marie Zakrzewska, a pioneer in opening the way for women to enter the medical profession, opened the nucleus of the New England Hospital for Women and Children in Boston. She served as physician, administrator and teacher of two generations of women doctors and nurses until 1899. She was also active in the abolitionist and women's rights movements.

1862-
1863

Both the "Polish Brigade" and the "Polish Legion" saw significant action in the Virginia and Gettysburg campaigns.

1863

Poles once more rebelled against Russian rule. Henry Kalussowski acted as their principle agent in the United States while the Polish Committee in New York City attempted to unify the exile community and rally support among native Americans. The Committee also published Echo z Polski (The Echo of Poland), the first Polish-language newspaper in the Western Hemisphere, during 1863-1864. The Union government favored Russia in the conflict in order to strengthen its international position against the Confederacy. The insurrection failed in 1864.

1864

Anton Smarszewski-Shermann and Peter Kiolbassa formed the mutual aid society of St. Stanislaus Kostka in Chicago. It lapsed after a few months but was the prototype of the many local insurance societies which later developed among Poles. When it was revived two years later it played a major part in founding the first Polish church in Chicago and in giving solid form to the Polish American Community.

1865

It is uncertain how many Poles participated in the Civil War, but Miecislaus Haiman estimated 5,000-4,000 for the Union, 1,000 for the Confederacy, or 16% of the total Polish American population. This was slightly higher than the overall national participation. There were at least 20 captains, 2 colonels (Joseph Karge and Wlodzimierz Krzyzanowski who were breveted brigadiers) and one brigadier-general (Albin Schoepf) of Polish descent in the Union Army. There were several captains and one colonel (Valerian Sulakowski) of Polish descent among the Confederates.

1866

Speaking for the American Catholic Church, the second Council of Baltimore decreed that priests who knew a foreign language should be placed in seaboard towns in order to serve immigrants in their mother tongue. The Council also encouraged teaching prospective priests the languages of immigrant groups among whom they might work.

Father Adolph Bakanowski, a member of the Polish Order of Resurrectionists, began four years of mission work in Texas. His memoirs, published in Poland in 1916, throw important light upon early Polish settlements in the United States. The Resurrectionists were, hencforth, a powerful factor in the Polish American community.

The St. Stanislaus Kostka Society was revived in Chicago with the formation of a parish and loyalty to the Catholic church among its chief objectives. At about the same time the Gmina Polska (The Polish Commune) was organized. It stood for more secular ideals--greater lay power in the church, support for an independent Polish homeland--and illustrated the basic division in the early movement to organize the Polish American community.

1867

St. Stanislaus Kostka church, the mother church among Chicago Poles, came into existence. It reflected the rapid growth in Polish immigration in the decade after the Civil War. Most of these immigrants came from Prussian-occupied sections of Poland. The parish was divided by the bitter quarrel between the clerical and secular factions.

1868   What was probably the first Polish school in America
        was established in St. Stanislaus parish in Milwaukee.
        The Polish school system became one of the most im-
        portant components of the Catholic parochial school system.

1870   The International Bridge over the Niagara river was be-
        gun under the direction of Casimir Gzowski, a Canadian
        Polish engineer and pioneer railroad builder.

        Joseph Karge was appointed to the chair of continental
        European languages and literature at Princeton College,
        a post he occupied until his death in 1892.

        Orzel Polski (The Polish Eagle), the second Polish-lan-
        guage newspaper in the United States, began publication
        in Washington, Missouri. While it had a short life, it
        was the prototype of future Polish American newspapers,
        serving the masses of Polish people and their needs in
        America. Ignacy Wendzinski, one of its editors, was typi-
        cal of the later Polish American newspaperman who com-
        bined the roles of editor, business manager and compositor.

1871   The clerical party, led by the Resurrectionists and Peter
        Kiolbassa, won complete control over St. Stanislaus Kostka
        parish in Chicago.

        The formation of the Kosciuszko Society in Philadelphia
        marked another effort to begin the unification of Polish
        colonies throughout the country.

1872   John Barzynski, an important publicist and promoter of
        the conservative Catholic cause among Polish Americans,
        arrived in the United States.

        The St. Joseph Society, directed by the old Gmina Polska
        leadership, was founded in Chicago to establish the new
        Holy Trinity church near St. Stanislaus Kostka.

1873   John Barzynski and Father Theodore Gieryk founded what
        later became known as the Polish Roman Catholic Union
        of America, the second largest Polish American fraternal
        organization. Its headquarters, at first in Detroit, were
        soon moved to Chicago.

        Wladyslaw Dyniewicz began his career in Chicago as a
        publisher and secular leader among Polish Americans.

Father John Pitass and the local St. Stanislaus society founded and led St. Stanislaus Bishop and Martyr parish in Buffalo, the first landmark in the development of one of America's largest Polish communities.

1874   The formation of the parish of St. Stanislaus Bishop and Martyr in New York City signaled the emergence formally of the Polish Catholic community in that city.

Father Vincent Barzynski, a Resurrectionist, became pastor of St. Stanislaus Kostka parish in Chicago. He was the spiritual and social leader of Chicago Poles as well as of his parish, the largest Polish congregation in the country, until his death in 1899. He also worked to bring the nearby Holy Trinity parish under the control of St. Stanislaus.

At the request of Joseph Dabrowski, then pastor of the Polish settlement in Polonia, Wisconsin, the first Sisters of the Congregation of St. Felix arrived in the United States to begin their American mission. They became the largest and most important Polish sisterhood in America.

1875   The decision of the third convention of the Polish Roman Catholic Union to remain an organization for Roman Catholics alone renewed discussion about creating a supraterritorial association of all American Poles.

1876   Henry Sienkiewicz, the renowned Polish novelist of later years, arrived in the United States for a stay of nearly two years. He spent most of his time in California. The American tour provided material for eight short stories and several journalistic accounts of native and Polish Americans.

Leon Jastremski, second generation American and former captain in the Confederate Army, was elected mayor of Baton Rouge, Louisiana, an office he held until 1882. He was a member of the conservative Democratic faction which "redeemed" the state from Radical Republican rule in 1876.

1877   Helena Modjeska made her American stage debut in San Francisco. She began a long career (until 1907) in the American theater where she was best known for her performances in Shakespeare's plays.

The Felicians (the Sisters of St. Felix) took charge of the St. Joseph Immigration Center on Ellis Island, New York. The Center had been founded by Polish clergy to aid newly arrived Polish immigrants.

1879

Agaton Giller, a Polish exile then in Switzerland, published "An Open Letter to the Poles in America" in the Polish American press. It stimulated new efforts to create a national association of Polish Americans.

1880

Ten Polish residents of Philadelphia, the same men who had founded the Kosciuszko Society earlier, met at the home of Julius Andrzejkowicz to discuss relief for their Polish brethren in Silesia. They realized that a union of local societies would have made it easier to collect contributions. Following a discussion of Agaton Giller's ideas, they formed what became the first lodge in the Polish National Alliance, the largest Polish American organization. The purposes of the Alliance were 1) restoration of an independent Poland and 2) assistance to the Polish immigrant in every aspect of his life in the United States.

1882

The Felicians Sisters established their headquarters in the more centrally situated area of Detroit.

As the Polish National Alliance grew, an era of extreme tension opened between it and the Polish Roman Catholic Union. On the grounds that it was open to any Pole, the Polish clergy argued that it threatened the faith of the immigrants and tried to force Catholics out of the Alliance.

1884

The third Council of the American Roman Catholic Church at Baltimore renewed its decrees of 1866 with respect to the immigrant. It also directed that migrant women and children receive special care.

Father Joseph Dabrowski won official approval from the Bishop of Detroit for his plan to establish a Polish seminary in that city.

1885

Construction of the (Polish) Seminary of SS. Cyril and Methodius began in Detroit.

At the request of Bishop Feehan and Father Barzynski of Chicago, the Sisters of the Holy Family of Nazareth began their mission in the United States. They first took charge of the parish school and of some orphans in St. Josaphat's parish and eventually became the second largest congregation of Polish American nuns.

Unusual claims for death benefits, an important feature in the appeal of the Polish National Alliance, put the organization's treasury into deficit and brought on a major financial crisis.

1886

The Polish Seminary opened its doors to students in Detroit.

Both the Polish Roman Catholic Union and the Polish National Alliance put their finances in order by adopting a pro rata system of life insurance. Their insurance programs bound many, quite different people together through self-interest and led the two fraternals into a period of sustained growth. The conflict between them subsided somewhat after this year.

Erazmus Jerzmanowski -- pioneer in the American gas industry, millionaire and philanthropist -- made a final effort to integrate all Polish American organizations. He was unsuccessful.

1887

Father John Pitass founded the newspaper The Pole in America (Polak w Ameryce) in Buffalo. It became an influential organ of conservative Catholic opinion, especially after becoming a daily in 1895. In Chicago, Father Vincent Barzynski and others founded the Polish Publications Association to support the same viewpoint.

Poles were now numerous enough in the anthracite coal industry of Pennsylvania to become a significant factor in the labor disturbances in the fields in 1887-1888.

1888

The Felician Sisters opened their first home for the aged, St. Mary's in Manitowac, Wisconsin.

Poles scored two breakthroughs in local politics. August Kowalski, a Republican supported by the Polish National Alliance, defeated Peter Kiolbassa, an organizer of the Polish Roman Catholic Union, to become Chicago's first Polish alderman. Stanley Kunz, a Democrat, won election to the state legislature from the thirteenth district in Chicago, the first step in a career which took him to the United States Congress. Organization politics became an important vehicle for Poles in their assimilation to and mobility upwards in American society.

Michael Kruszka began publication of the Polish Courier (Kuryer Polski) in Milwaukee, the first successful Polish daily newspaper in the United States. It spoke for progressive, nationalist opinion, sometimes accused of being leftist and anti-clerical.

1889   Anthony Paryski began publication of America-Echo (Am-
            eryka-Echo), one of the most widely read Polish American
            newspapers, in Toledo, Ohio.

1890   The Polish Publications Association founded the Chicago
            Daily News (Dziennik Chicagoski), an influential organ of
            Polish Catholic opinion.

            As a result of a division within the Polish National Alli-
            ance, the Polish Union of America was established with
            headquarters in Wilkes-Barre, Pennsylvania.

            Victor Bardonski, a Democrat, won a term of office as a
            Cook County (Illinois) commissioner -- a "first" for Polish
            Americans in a major county-wide election.

1891   Poles won their first general municipal office when Peter
            Kiolbassa was elected Chicago's city treasurer as a Demo-
            crat.

1893   The long-simmering feud between Father Barzynski and
            the nationalists of Holy Trinity parish in Chicago was
            brought to an end in favor (in effect) of the nationalists.
            The Apostolic Delegate, the American representative of
            the Pope, sanctioned the appointment of Father Casimir
            Sztuczko, a Holy Cross Father from Notre Dame, as
            pastor of the parish.

            Father Francis Hodur -- recently ordained a Roman
            Catholic priest in Scranton, Pennsylvania -- undertook a
            mission to Rome to secure a greater voice for Poles in
            the American Catholic church.

            The Polish Commercial-Geographical Society was founded
            in Poznan and, the following year, in Lwow in order to
            collect statistical data on industrial conditions in various
            parts of the world. It supplied basic information for
            people planning to emigrate.

            The Polish sokol movement -- athletic-fraternal
            societies -- began in the United States.

1894   The "Hakata" was formed in the Prussian-annexed part
            of Poland. It was a powerful, private organization for
            Germanizing Prussian Poland.

            Father John Pitass was appointed Dean and Vicar-General
            for all the Poles in the diocese of Buffalo. Although the

appointment was not renewed when a new bishop took office in 1896, the Buffalo Poles continued to regard Pitass as their Dean.

The Polish Bernadine Sisters began their work in the United States. They were most active in the northeastern states.

A controversy, one of several that led to the formation of the Polish National Catholic Church, began in St. Hedwige's parish in Chicago. Parish leaders criticized the financial management of their pastor, John Barzynski (brother to Father Vincent) and sought to take control of the parish from him. They rallied around the assistant pastor, Anthony Kozlowski.

A major depression in the American economy and an improvement in the condition of peasants in eastern Germany led to the decline of emigration from German-controlled portions of Poland.

1895   The struggle in St. Hedwige's in Chicago intensified, leading to the dismissal of Kozlowski, violent conflict and a secession from the parish by the critics who, nevertheless, appealed to Rome to uphold their position.

The Alliance of Poles in America, a largely regional fraternal insurance organization, was established in Ohio.

1896   The First Polish Catholic Congress in America was held in Buffalo under the leadership of Father Pitass to discuss the problems of Polish American Catholics -- schisms within parish churches, the absence of bishops of Polish descent, the relationship between church and secular organizations, the Polish seminary, and the Polish American press. Two priests were delegated to present these problems to church authorities at the Vatican.

Polish American voters, though not yet numerous, probably supported William Jennings Bryan and the Democratic party in the national election of this year. Poles had gravitated, probably, toward the Democratic party since the early years of their mass migration in the 1870's.

1897   Father Anthony Kozlowski was consecrated a bishop by the head of the Swiss Old Catholic Church in Berne, sealing the breach between his followers and the Roman Catholic church. He returned to the United States, the first Polish

and Old Catholic bishop in North America, with jurisdiction over a scattering of Polish American groups.

Spontaneous demonstrations and strikes by Poles seeking
economic justice in the hard coal fields of Pennsylvania
encouraged the United Mine Workers to attempt to organize
the new immigrants here. At Lattimer, sixty strikers --
all of them Poles, Slovaks or Lithuanians -- were killed or
wounded in the course of one demonstration.

The Polish Colonization Society was founded in Lwow
(Poland).

1898   The Polish Women's Alliance was begun in Chicago. It
        was a major step in the evolution of an independent role
        for women in Polish America.

1899   Polish workers renewed their aggressive pursuit of econo-
        mic justice in the anthracite coal fields. As in 1897, they
        were in advance of union leaders and won important con-
        cessions. They also took part in the strikes of 1900 and
        1902 when the union made further gains for the miners.

1900   After twenty-five years in the United States, the Felician
        sisters counted some 400 members in their ranks and
        staffed schools and other institutions in sixteen states.

        The Polish Beneficial Association, an insurance fraternal
        oriented to the Middle Atlantic States, was founded in Penn-
        sylvania.

1901   The Second Polish Catholic Congress convened in Buffalo
        in conjunction with the Pan-American Exposition. It dis-
        cussed the issues that had been raised at the First Congress
        and decided to send two delegates, Father Pitass and Father
        Waclaw Kruszka of Wisconsin, to present the position of the
        Polish immigration to church authorities in Rome.

        Bishop Anthony Kozlowski sought to establish inter-com-
        munion between his followers and the Protestant Episcopal
        Church in the United States. His request was turned down
        by the Episcopalians.

        School children in Wrzesnia, Prussian Poland, struck
        against the Germanization of their schools. Their protest
        evoked widespread sympathy among American Poles who
        saw in it a parallel to their resistence to the Americani-
        zation of their parochial schools and churches.

1903
The Felician sisters opened the St. Felix Home in Buffalo as a residence for young working women.

The Polish National Alliance of Brooklyn, an insurance fraternal focusing on metropolitan New York City, was founded.

Father Kruszka and Rowland Mahany, a Buffalo attorney and congressman, substituting for Father Pitass, began their delegation to Rome seeking greater representation and power for Poles in the American Catholic church. Their mission lasted until 1904.

1904
After several years of lobbying by Polish American organizations the United States Congress enacted legislation authorizing a monument to Tadeusz Kosciuszko near the Capitol in Washington, D. C.

The Polish Daily News (Dziennik Polski), a major and long-lived Polish-language newspaper, began publication in Detroit.

Polish Americans probably supported the Republican Theodore Roosevelt in the presidential campaign against the conservative Democrat Alton Parker. They were influenced by the argument that the Square Deal meant steady employment and fair treatment for workers, by Roosevelt's good relations with the Catholic church and by Roosevelt's support for Polish representation in the American Catholic hierarchy. However, they seem to have remained largely Democratic in local politics.

1905
John Smulski, formerly city attorney in Chicago, became state treasurer of Illinois, a "first" for Poles in statewide elective office.

Father Waclaw Kruszka began publication of The History of Poland in America (Historya Polska w Ameryce). Although controversial and not always accurate, it was the first large-scale attempt to describe and synthesize the Polish experience in the United States.

Revolutionary disturbances in Russian Poland, growing out of social discontent and Russia's losses in war with Japan, evoked sympathy among American Poles but found them unprepared to deal with the situation in political terms.

Pope Pius X sent the Polish Archbishop Albin Symon to the United States to investigate the complaints and condition of Catholic Poles. The archbishop visited the major Polish American communities and met President Roosevelt who supported the claims of the Polish clergy to representation in the American hierarchy. Symon made a report to the pope but there were no immediate consequences.

1907   Father Francis Hodur was consecrated a bishop in the Dutch Old Catholic Church. The event marked the beginning of the episcopal hierarchy of the Polish National Catholic Church in the United States. The headquarters of the church were established in Scranton, Pennsylvania. After the death of Bishop Kozlowski in the same year, most of the twenty-three parishes under his jurisdiction joined Bishop Hodur's organization.

Polish Socialists in Chicago began publication of the People's Daily (Dziennik Ludowy). It became the organ of the Polish Socialist Party in America, a vigorous if small movement.

1908   The Polish Emigration Society was founded in Krakow in order to channel immigrant laborers into areas where they might find jobs.

The Polish National Alliance began publication in Chicago of its newspaper, Alliance Daily (Dziennik Zwiazkowy).

The Polish National Union of American, an insurance fraternal, was established in Scranton, Pennsylvania, under the auspices of the Polish National Catholic Church.

Father Paul Rhode was appointed auxiliary bishop of Chicago, becoming the first American Roman Catholic bishop of Polish descent. He later served as bishop of Green Bay, Wisconsin.

1909   Under its second rector, Witold Buhaczhowski, the Polish Seminary in Detroit moved to new quarters in nearby Orchard Lake. There it became the focus of a cluster of Polish American schools.

1910   American Poles gathered in Washington, D. C., in their largest national meeting thus far to witness the unveiling of monuments to Pulaski and Kosciuszko. The presence of representatives from Europe gave it a claim to

be the first world-wide congress of the Polish nation.
The event was also the occasion for commemorating the
500th anniversary of the battle of Grunwald in which Poland
had defeated the German Teutonic Knights -- an opportunity
for demonstrating strong anti-German and Polish nationalist feelings.

The Emigrants Protective Association was founded in Warsaw.

In what was the first fairly accurate count of Polish Americans, the United States census revealed that there were
937,884 Americans born in Poland and 725,924 native
Americans with one or both parents born in Poland.

1911   The Polish National Alliance opened an Emigrants Home
in New York City to assist newly arrived Polish immigrants.

The Association of the Sons of Poland, a regional insurance
fraternal, was established. It operated largely in New
Jersey.

1912   The Polish National Alliance opened an academy (later
Alliance College) in Cambridge Springs, Pennsylvania.

The ethnic Polish immigration to the United States reached
a peak of nearly 175,000 during the official year 1912-
1913. It was 14.6% of the total migration to the country.
Men outnumbered women two to one. As it had for the
past fifteen years, nearly all of this migration came from
Russian and Austrian occupied parts of Poland.

Polish Americans divided their votes among the major candidates for the presidency, possibly giving strongest support to Theodore Roosevelt. Their motives included a
recollection of Roosevelt's behavior as president and Woodrow Wilson's alleged hostility to newer immigrants.

At the call of the Central Board of the Falcons, all Polish
American organizations sent delegates to Pittsburgh on
December 12 to plan for the political future of Poland.
Out of the meeting grew the Committee for National
Defense, known as the KON from its Polish name (Komi-
tet Obrony Narodrowej). The KON was oriented to the
views of the Polish leader Joseph Pilsudski and the United
Independence parties. Thus, it was mildly socialist in
its program for a future Poland, pro-Austrian and anti-

Russian in attitude toward the major partition powers. As these views became clearer, the Committee came under sharp attack from the clergy.

1913   The first major split in the KON came within six months of its founding when the Polish Roman Catholic Union withdrew. Led by Bishop Rhode and other clergy, the PRCU formed the Polish National Council in America which allied itself with socially conservative and pro-Russian elements in Poland and in the exile community. It failed to unite all non-KON Groups, however, and soon weakened.

Spurred on by the Balkan wars and the talk of general war in Europe, the Falcons abandonned their usual routine of gymnastic exercises in their lodges and concentrated on basic military training. The shift in policy had parallels among European Poles.

The Felician sisters opened their first day nursery, Guardian Angel, in Buffalo.

1914   When war threatened between the United States and Mexico, the Falcons offered President Wilson the services of a thousand or more of their trained militia. The Army politely refused their offer.

Most of the remaining members of the KON withdrew during the first half of the year and set up separate organizations to deal with the possibility of Polish independence. On the eve of World War I, the Polish American community was divided in its approach to the future of the Polish question.

After the outbreak of war in Europe, American Poles formed a non-political Polish Central Relief Committee to aid victims in what became one of the chief battlegrounds. The committee was composed of the five major groups which had left the KON.

1915   Casimir Funk, scientist and pioneer in vitamin research, began his first extended stay in the United States.

Germany and Austria occupied most of Russian Poland during the summer.

1916   President Wilson proclaimed January 1st as Polish Relief Day. All donations (each Pole was supposed to give one day's wages) were given to the American Red Cross to aid war victims in Poland.

The Canadian War Office and leaders of the Polish Falcons of America concluded an agreement secretly in which Canada agreed to train a small cadre of Polish Americans for military service.

The pianist Ignacy Paderewski, Roman Dmowski and other European Polish leaders convinced the sponsors of the Polish Central Relief Committee to set up a National Department. As its political bureau, the National Department soon became the driving force in the Committee and a factor in the movement for Polish independence.

Polish Americans voted heavily for Woodrow Wilson for president. Their motives included Wilson's cooperation in plans for Polish relief, the support of Polish leaders like Paderewski who hoped Wilson would support Polish independence in the post-war settlement, the nativist tone of some Republican campaigning, and the positive attitude of the Democratic party to certain measures favoring the workingman.

1917   In a speech to the Senate on January 22, President Wilson supported "a united, independent and autonomous Poland" after the war. Polish and Polish American agitation helped create the atmosphere in which this declaration was possible.

At their annual convention, prior to American entry into the World War, the Falcons called for a force of 100,000 men to help Poland when the need arose.

Following the American declaration of war against Germany, Americans of Polish descent saw service in the nation's armed forces well out of proportion to their number in the total population. About 215,000 participated.

France set in motion plans to create a Polish Army on its soil and recognized the Polish National Committee in Switzerland as the spokesman for Polish interests. In the United States the National Department won the exclusive right to enlist men for the Polish army from among residents who were not yet citizens. The government also recognized the Department as the representative of the American Polish community.

Polish Army recruits were trained at Alliance College in Cambridge Springs, Pennsylvania, at Fort Niagara in New York and especially at a camp at Niagara-on-the-Lake in Canada. The first of them left for France in November. Efforts to provide for their welfare were made through such organizations as the new Polish White Cross.

1918

Wilson outlined American war aims, the Fourteen Points, in an address to Congress on January 8. The thirteenth point called for the establishment of an independent Poland, including territories with an indisputably Polish population, with free and secure access to the sea. While it appeared to support the objectives of Poles in Europe and America, Wilson's statement was ambiguous about the boundaries of the future Polish state.

American members of the Polish Army in France saw significant combat action for the first time in June and July. Their army never fought in the war as a separate, integrated unit. It was only in late September, shortly before the Armistice, that General Joseph Haller was confirmed as commander of the Polish Army in France.

American Poles met in Detroit during August for their most significant war-time convention. The supporters of the Polish National Committee (the Paderewski-Dmowski group) and the leaders of the National Department dominated the proceedings. Besides renewing their support for established Polish and Polish American war aims, the delegates launched a drive to raise ten million dollars for a special fund to aid Poland. For a number of reasons, among them the already heavy demands upon Polish Americans to contribute to the American and Polish war efforts, less than half of the ten million was raised before the end of the year.

John Kleczka was elected to the United States Congress from Milwaukee on the Republican ticket. However, about three-quarters of Polish American Congressmen since this first one have been Democrats.

William I. Thomas and Florian Znaniecki, an American and a Polish sociologist respectively, began publication of The Polish Peasant in Europe and America. Based largely on the letters and other documents of Polish peasants and immigrants, this multi-volume work was a landmark in the interpretation of peasant society and migration. It focused on the disruption of peasant communities under the

impact of economic modernization and migration and on the
reconstruction of the peasant community in more modern
form in the cities of the United States.

1919   Polish Americans tried to influence Wilson and the Paris
Peace Conference to grant Poland more favorable bounda-
ries at the expense of Germany. They were mostly unsuccessful, owing to the opposition of Great Britain, the
weakness of the Polish government and the confusion on
the eastern frontier of Poland.

Recruiting for the Polish Army was halted in the United
States in February. At that time the Army stood at 108,000
fighting men. American Poles had, since June 1917, recruited 40,000 men, accepted and trained 30,000, and sent
24,260 overseas to join its ranks.

General Haller's Polish Army arrived in Poland in April
to participate in the Polish-Russian war over boundaries
in eastern Europe. They never saw much action as a
group in Poland nor were they well-supplied. Besides,
American citizens in the Army began to petition for dis-
charge. Plans were made in the late summer to repatriate
the soldiers.

A major race riot in Chicago marked a major turning point
in relations between whites (including Poles) and Blacks
whose number had increased during the war era. The divi-
sions between the Blacks and the white ethnic groups hard-
ened appreciably.

The treatment of the Jewish minority in the new Poland
raised the question of Polish-Jewish relations anew for
American Poles.

A bitter strike in the steel industry, a major employer
of Poles, began in September. It ended by January in a
decisive defeat for organized labor.

The Association of the Sons of Poland and the Polish Union
in the United States began publication of the influential
Polish-language daily, The New World (Nowy Swiat), in
New York City.

1920   Polish Army veterans began to return to the United States
in April in American Army transports. Use of the trans-
ports was authorized by a law sponsored by Congressman
Kleczka and Senator James Wadsworth. About 19,000 men
returned within a year to a cool and disappointing welcome

from their compatriots.   Most efforts to help them afterwards were inadequate.   The veterans formed their own
fraternal organization.

The Polish minister to the Vatican intervened with the
Pope on behalf of Polish American clergy to secure more
American bishops of Polish descent.   His action brought
a strong protest from the leaders of the American Catholic church.

Stanley Coveleski (Kowalewski) reached the high point of
his career as a pitcher for the baseball Cleveland Indians,
winning 24 games in the regular season and three in the
World Series.   Like many other second generation Polish
Americans, he achieved a measure of economic success
and recognition through the mass entertainment industry --
professional sports, collegiate football, films.

The United States Census showed that there were 1,303,351
native Americans with one or both parents born in Poland
and 1,139,978 Americans who had been born in Poland.

The post-war re-migration of Polish Americans to Poland
rose to 42,207 in 1920-1921.   It dropped to 31,004 in 1921-
1922 and fell off sharply thereafter.

1921   An economic depression, though brief, adversely affected
the position of the American worker.   Poles took part in
a major strike in Chicago's stockyards late in the year
and early in 1922; it was unsuccessful and, besides, had
strong racial overtones.   During the 1920's and early
thirties, the membership of the United Mine Workers fell
from 500,000 to 150,000.   Except in textiles and coal mining, however, real wages and per capita income rose after
1923.

Congress enacted the Emergency Quota Act limiting the
number of immigrants entering the United States each
year to three percent of the population of each nationality
group living in the United States in 1910.   It sharply
reduced the number of Polish immigrants entering the
United States.

John Smulski, the president of the Polish National Department, reported that American Poles altogether had chan-
nelled over $200,000,000.00 into all aspects of the Polish
cause.   This figure did not include the $67,000,000.00 in
Liberty Bonds which they had bought.

Most of the 5,000 Polish Army veterans who had at first thought to remain in Poland returned to the United States with the aid of the Polish government. Such events and the declining activity of the National Department revealed a rapid withdrawal from direct participation in Polish affairs and greater concern with the welfare of Polish Americans.

Professor Joseph T. Tykociner, a native of Poland, gave the first public demonstration of sound-on-film movies at the University of Illinois.

1924   The Immigration Act of 1924 made the immigrant quota system permanent, restricting admissions to two percent of each national group in United States in 1890. The overall quota was 164,447 (later 150,000). Poland's quota was reduced from 30,977 to 5,982, an example of the discrimination against east and south European immigrants on which the act was founded. The law illustrated the fear of many native Americans that foreigners could not be assimilated to American life; a fear which had led to vigorous efforts to Americanize immigrants in the previous decade. The law also reflected the belief that American workers needed protection against the competition of foreign laborers.

1925   The Kosciuszko Foundation was established in New York City under the direction of Stephen Mizwa with the aid of Henry Noble MacCracken, president of Vassar College, and Samuel M. Vauclain, president of the Baldwin Locomotive Works. The Foundation sought to promote better cultural relations between the United States and Poland in a variety of ways: supporting the exchange of scholars, professors and lecturers between the two countries; granting financial aid to Polish students in American universities and American students in Polish universities; subsidizing publications, cultural events, exhibits and concerts which would increase understanding of Polish culture; and (after 1939) by aiding refugee scholars from Poland.

Polish Americans experimented, unsuccessfully in the long run, with a system of Polish Welfare Councils which were to unite them locally and nationally in pursuit of their common goals.

1926   The Polish Arts Club was organized in Chicago. It was the first of many such clubs devoted to promoting an understanding of Polish culture and stimulating the cultural achievement of Polish Americans. Most of them were formed by members of the rising generation of university students or graduates and often found homes on college campuses.

1928

Polish Americans once more gave very strong support to the Democratic national ticket, now led by Al Smith of New York. Smith's Catholic-urban-immigrant background, opposition to Prohibition, and sympathy to the workingman gave him his special appeal to Polish Americans. The election also witnessed the growing political strength of the second generation of Poles in the United States and thus represented their assimilation to American life.

The Trumpeter of Krakow by Eric Kelly won the Newberry Medal as the outstanding American literary work for children. Kelly's book, which a Kosciuszko Foundation grant had helped make possible, became probably the most popular introduction to Polish culture for American children.

1929

Marie Sklodowska Curie, the renowned Polish physicist and chemist, visited the United States for the second time.

Late in the year, the United States entered a financial crisis leading to the Great Depression -- an event which had a powerful effect upon the economic status and outlook of a generation of Polish Americans. Among other things it made them more receptive to the labor movement and to the growth of the welfare state.

After several years of preparation the semi-official First World Congress of Poles Abroad was held in Warsaw. It was called to discuss the problems of the kinds of Poles who lived abroad and how these Poles stood in relation to the Polish homeland. A formal organization, the Council of the Organization of Poles from Abroad, grew out of its deliberations.

1930

The United States Census revealed that 1,268,583 Americans had been born in Poland and that 2,073,615 native Americans (the largest number ever) had had one or both parents born in Poland.

The Polish language press stood at eighty-four, including fifteen daily newspapers, at the end of its most flourishing decade.

1931

The Father Justin Rosary Hour began a long run on United States and Canadian radio. Forty years later this Polish Catholic devotional program was heard on 42 radio stations and had an audience of over two million.

Anton Cermak, a Czech American, was elected mayor of Chicago with the support of most white ethnic groups (including Poles), the labor movement and liberals. He also set out to win support among Blacks, anticipating the New Deal Democratic coalition which emerged under Franklin Roosevelt and governed the country until 1953 and from 1961 to 1969.

1934

The Second Congress of Poles from Abroad was held in Warsaw. Statisticians estimated that nearly eight million Poles, about 22% of the total in the world, lived outside Poland. The Congress created a more active permanent organization -- the World Alliance of Poles Abroad -- which tried to sustain interest in the mother country among all Poles and to give special aid to Poles who lived in countries adjacent to Poland. The role of Polish America was defined as mainly economic -- a source of trade, maritime traffic, remittances and capital investment.

1935

The Polish Roman Catholic Union established its Polish Museum in Chicago and appointed the newspaper editor Miecislaus Haiman as its first curator. Under Haiman, the Museum and Archives of the PRCU became the most important collection of Polish American materials in the United States.

1936

Miecislaus Szymczak, a Chicago economist and lawyer, was appointed a governor of the Federal Reserve System -- the most significant federal appointment a Polish American had achieved to that time.

The Committee for Industrial Organization (C. I. O.) began to organize the motor and steel industries and to revive the labor movement in coal mining. Within five years, unions in each of these industries -- each with large Polish memberships -- had grown spectacularly and won recognition from all major employers.

1937

The Polish Arts Club published an important anthology of Polish American poetry in Chicago. About half of the book was written in English, evidence of the assimilation of the younger generation of Polish Americans.

Polish Americans sponsored the first Pulaski Day Parade on Fifth Avenue in New York City, a major symbolic event climaxing a decade of effort to make the anniversary of Pulaski's death a national holiday. This choice, instead of the more traditional Polish holidays revealed the degree of Americanization of Poles in the country.

The Felician sisters opened their first hospital, St. Mary's in Centralia, Illinois.

Clara Swieczkowska, a Detroit social worker, founded the Polish League of Social Activities in the U. S. A. and was elected its first president.

1938   The Felician sisters took charge of the Catholic Settlement House in Toronto, Ontario.

1939   The Polish Arts and Cultural Clubs began the practice of holding annual, national conventions.

As a major war crisis developed in Europe during the spring, following the German occupation of all of Czechoslovakia, American Poles began to gather money for the defense of Poland, commonly regarded as the next object of German pressure.

After the defeat of Poland by Germany in the opening campaign of World War II and the partition of the country between Germany and Russia in September, American Poles concentrated on the relief of war victims and refugees. The Polish American Council under Dean Francis Swietlik of Marquette University was their principal coordinating agency. Polish American opinion supported the Polish Government-in-Exile headed by General Wladyslaw Sikorski, first in Paris and later in London.

1940   The defeat of Poland followed by the fall of France in 1940 led many Polish artists (like the musician Wanda Landowska), scholars and scientists to settle in the United States.

Frank Piasecki founded an engineering research group which was the forerunner of the P-V Engineering Forum (incorporated in 1943), the Piasecki Helicopter Corporation (incorporated in 1946) and, finally, an important division of the Boeing Corporation. Piasecki's enterprises played an important role in helicopter design and production in the 1940's.

According to the Federal Census, 1,912,380 native Americans had one or both parents born in Poland; 993,479 Americans had been born in Poland itself, a significant decline in the Polish-born population since 1930.

1941   The Felician sisters took charge of the Bishop Duffy Child Center in Brant, New York, where they ran a summer program of recreation and education for the children of migrant farm workers. They also opened a unique Catholic American institution, the St. Rita Home for Mentally Deficient Children in Getzville, New York.

Stanley Musial began his major league baseball career with the St. Louis Cardinals, winning his league's Most Valuable Player award three times (1943, 1946, 1948) and establishing numerous hitting records before his retirement in 1963. He then became a vice-president in the Cardinals' organization.

The first of three Polish American Homiletic Congresses was held at the Polish Seminary at Orchard Lake.

The United States entered the war directly against Japan and Germany in December. The Polish American contribution to the war once more exceeded its proportion of the total population.

Refugee scholars, under the chairmanship of Oscar Halecki, organized the Polish Institute of Arts and Sciences in America. Growing out of an association formed in the previous year, the Institute was conceived of as a branch of the Polish Academy of Arts and Sciences. It had three objectives: to provide Polish scholars with a center and a means to sustain their identity as Poles; to promote Polish education; and to increase understanding of Polish culture in the United States.

1942

The Felician sisters opened a Psychological and Child Guidance Clinic in Buffalo to diagnose and treat emotional disturbances in children.

Slavic communities in the United States, represented by about 2,500 delegates, met in Detroit during April to form the American Slav Congress. A substantial Polish American delegation attended and two Polish Americans were elected officers: Leo Krzycki, a left-wing labor leader from Milwaukee, as president; and Blair Gunther, a Pittsburgh judge and civic leader, as chairman of the board. The Congress was attacked for supporting the Soviet Union and within two years most of its Polish members had withdrawn.

A delegation of Polish Americans led by Maximilian Wegrzynek, publisher of Nowy Swiat in New York City, went to the White House where they appealed for a restoration of Poland within its pre-war boundaries at any future peace settlement. Soon afterwards, many of the same leaders organized the militant National Committee of Americans of Polish Descent (KNAPP, after its Polish initials). It was strongly opposed to any attempts, including those of the London government of Sikorski, to compromise Polish war aims in favor of the Soviet Union.

With Miecislaus Haiman and Oscar Halecki providing the original stimulus, the Polish Institute of Artsand Sciences organized the Commission for Research on Polish Immigration. The commission began to publish Polish American Studies in 1944 and gradually evolved into the autonomous Polish American Historical Association.

1943   Polish scholars who had fled to the United States as a result of the war established the Joseph Pilsudski Institute of America in New York City to promote research into and understanding of modern Polish history and politics.

Charges that the Soviet Union had executed thousands of Polish officers in the Katyn Forest near Smolensk in 1940 led to a complete break between the Polish Government-in Exile and Russia. It also tended to confirm the views of the KNAPP group and led to an increase of anti-Soviet feeling among American Poles. The death of Prime Minister Sikorski in July, however, stilled some of the criticism of the Government-in-Exile among Polish Americans.

Polish American Catholic bishops and priests initiated the Catholic League for Religious Assistance to Poland. At the end of 1959, it had dispensed over four and one-half million dollars in relief or religious aid to Poles in Poland and elsewhere in Europe.

War Relief Services of the National Catholic Welfare Conference (the national organization of Roman Catholic bishops) began relief work among Poles displaced by the World War. Between December 1943 and June 1946, it distributed more than two and one-half million dollars in aid to Polish refugees in the Middle East.

Leo Krzycki, Father Stanislaus Orlemanski, a little known priest from Springfield, Massachusetts, and Oscar Lange, an economist at the University of Chicago who had been naturalized as an American citizen in 1943, formed the the Kosciuszko Polish Patriotic League in Detroit. It favored the Soviet position on Poland but had very little influence among American Poles.

1944

Father Orlemanski and Professor Lange visited Russia in
early May and conferred with Stalin, hoping that a Soviet
government would not be imposed upon Poland as it was being liberated from German rule. Their action and their
support of the Soviet Union on Poland's eastern boundary
stirred up a vigorous, negative reaction from American
Poles.

At the call of leaders of the major Polish fraternals and
civic organizations (including Poles in the KNAPP and the
American Slav Congress), about 4,000 delegates met in
Buffalo for the founding convention of the Polish American
Congress. Charles Rozmarek, the president of the Polish
National Alliance, was elected president of the Congress'
permanent organization. The Congress was preoccupied
with two issues: concessions by the Western Allies to
Russia on the eastern boundary of Poland which had been
discussed at the Teheran Conference in the previous year;
and the nature of the post-war government and international
position of Poland.

Roosevelt and Churchill appealed to Stalin to drop supplies
to insurgents in Warsaw during August or to allow American and British planes to do so and then land on Soviet
soil. Stalin refused both requests. Just prior to this he had
allowed the formation of a pro-Communist (Lublin) Polish
government in Soviet occupied territory. American Poles
became further disenchanted with the American policy of
cooperation with the Soviet Union.

The opinions of American Poles, especially as it was an
election year, had some effect (but not a decisive one) upon
the Polish policy of the Roosevelt administration. On
October 11, Charles Rozmarek and other leaders of the
Polish-American Congress met Roosevelt and took a strongly anti-Soviet line with him; Roosevelt responded in general
terms and did not commit himself clearly on the Polish
question. On the eve of the election, Rozmarek endorsed
the president for re-election. Polish Americans voted for
him overwhelmingly once again.

War Relief Services began negotiations through UNRRA
(United Nations Relief and Rehabilitation Administration),
the primary relief agency, to undertake programs of its
own in Poland.

1945

After lengthy discussions, the Yalta Conference of Allied
wartime leaders (Roosevelt, Churchill, Stalin) significantly advanced plans for the future of Poland. Russia was to
retain the territory she had occupied in September 1939,

and Poland, which was to be compensated with German territory, was allowed to occupy southern East Prussia and eastern Germany up to the Oder and Neisse rivers. The Polish (Lublin) government was to be reorganized on a broader basis and free elections were to be held in the country after the war. After tentative early approval, these decisions were criticized strongly by Polish American leaders who felt that Poland had been "betrayed" by the western powers.

At the San Francisco Conference to draft the Charter of the United Nations Organization, leaders of the Polish American Congress lobbied actively in behalf of the London Government-in-Exile. Working through Senator Arthur Vandenberg, they were able to prevent the seating of the Lublin Polish Government. However, the United States recognized a reorganized Polish Government and withdrew recognition from the London Government, another substantial defeat for the viewpoint of Polish American leaders.

Several Poles contributed to the development of atomic weapons, notably the mathmatician Stanislaus Ulam who had emigrated to the United States in 1935.

War Relief Services inaugurated its major relief program in Poland late in the year. It worked through the Polish Catholic agency Caritas until 1950 when the Polish government discontinued most of its operations.

1946   Polish American leaders (Charles Rozmarek, Oscar Halecki, Ignatius Nurkiewicz) raised the Polish question with Western leaders at the Paris Conference of Great Power Foreign Ministers. Their protests fell on increasingly deaf ears in the American government.

Prime-Bishop Hodur of the Polish National Catholic Church entered into inter-communion with the Protestant Episcopal Church of America. The General Synod of the Polish church failed, however, to accept full communion between the two bodies.

1948   The Polish National Catholic Church joined the World Council of Churches, having earlier become a member of the National Council of Churches in the United States.

Sixteen Polish American cultural clubs formed the American Council of Polish Cultural Clubs which held its first convention in the following year.

After several steps by President Truman to admit persons
displaced by the war to the United States, the Congress
enacted the Displaced Persons Act. Under this and later
refugee relief laws, 151,978 persons born in Poland were
admitted to the country. They were assisted by various
Catholic relief and Polish American organizations. They
added a significant new strain to Polish America, possess-
ing a different and more recent view of Poland, often better
educated and holding a higher socio-economic status than
the earlier Polish immigration.

Polish Americans continued to support the Democratic
party, voting heavily in favor of President Truman. Despite their disappointments over the disposition of the
Polish question, Polish Americans were influenced by the
administration's support for relief of Poland and refugees,
by Truman's increasingly anti-communist foreign policy
in 1947-1948, and by the heritage of the New Deal's social
programs.

Madonna College, conducted by the Felician sisters near
Detroit, was incorporated as a senior college. Twenty
years later, in 1968-1969, it had an enrollment of about
725 students.

1949   Joseph Mruk was elected mayor of Buffalo on the Republi-
            can ticket -- the first mayor of Polish descent in a major
            American city.

1950   According to the United States Census, 861,184 Americans
            claimed Poland as their country of birth; 1,925,015 had
            one or both parents born in Poland. The decline in the
            number of foreign-born Poles and the relative stability
            in the size of the second generation suggested that a third
            generation of Polish Americans was becoming a more im-
            portant segment of the population.

1952   The presidential campaign of Dwight Eisenhower witnessed
            the culmination of the movement to prove that Poland and,
            by inference, the interests of Polish America had been
            "betrayed" by the Democratic administration during the
            war. The Republicans made sizeable inroads into the
            Polish Democratic vote, though it is not clear that foreign
            policy was the main reason. Once in office, in 1953, the
            Republican administration abandonned campaign promises
            to "roll back the Iron Curtain" in eastern Europe.

1953   Bishop Leon Grochowski succeeded as prime-bishop of the
            Polish National Catholic Church upon the death of Bishop
            Hodur.

After nearly eighty years in the United States the Felician sisters reported a membership of 3,620 sisters in twenty-seven states, the District of Columbia, Ontario and Brazil -- more than four times the size of the mother community in Poland. They operated 250 elementary schools, twenty-eight high schools, three junior colleges and one senior college with an enrollment of over 85,000 students. Since 1874, they had given a temporary home to more than 87,400 children in their orphanages and other institutions.

1954   The Sisters of the Holy Family opened Holy Family College in Philadelphia as a four-year liberal arts institution.

Edmund Muskie was elected governor of Maine as a Democrat. The son of an immigrant from Poland, he was the first American of Polish descent to achieve this office. His subsequent campaigns for senator, vice-president and president were also "firsts" for Polish Americans in politics.

Prime-Bishop Grochowski strengthened the links of doctrine and liturgy between the Polish National Catholic Church and the Old Catholics of Europe. A bishop of the Protestant Episcopal Church of America participated in the consecration of a Polish National Catholic bishop.

1955   A congress in Warsaw led to the formation of the Society for Relations with the Emigration -- the "Polonia" society -- and effort to re-establish cultural contact with Poles throughout the world.

Seventy years after beginning their mission in the United States, the Sisters of the Holy Family had over 2,500 members in eighteen states. They staffed ten hospitals, eighty-one elementary schools, fifteen secondary schools, seven post-secondary schools, and two colleges.

1956   Dwight Eisenhower won 36.5% of the vote in areas with heavy concentrations of Polish Americans in his successful bid to be re-elected president.

The Polish Institute of Arts and Sciences in America published the first issue of The Polish Review -- an important scholarly publication devoted to Polish culture.

1957   With the strong support of Polish American organizations, the United States extended large credits for economic development to Poland. The amount, however, was less than a third of the 300 million dollars the Poles had asked for. The extension of aid reflected improved relations between the two countries growing out of a change in the Polish government and liberalization of Polish life in 1956.

1958   Edmund Muskie was elected United States Senator from Maine.

Random House published A Glass Rose by Richard Bankowsky -- one of the few substantial novels by a Polish American making use of Polish American material.

1960   Poles contributed heavily to the erection of the Polish Chapel of Our Lady of Czestochowa in the National Shrine of the Immaculate Conception in Washington, D. C.

Stanislaus Skrowaczewski, the Polish composer and conductor, was appointed musical director of the Minneapolis Symphony (since renamed the Minnesota Orchestra).

The Felician sisters established Villa Maria College as a junior college in Buffalo.

John F. Kennedy won over eighty percent of the vote in areas of heaviest Polish American population in his campaign for the presidency. He reversed the tendency of more Poles to vote Republican in the 1950's. Twelve Polish Americans were elected to the 87th Congress -- the largest number to that time and afterwards; ten of them were Democrats.

Near the end of the year the White House announced that Poland would be given most favored nation status in American foreign trade.

The federal census showed that there were 747,000 foreign-born American Poles and 2,031,000 of foreign or mixed Polish parentage. The Polish National Catholic Church reported 282,000 members in 162 churches served by 151 pastors. Presumably, most of the rest of the Polish Americans were at least formally Roman Catholic.

1961   The Mazowsze, the Polish Folk Song and Dance Company of Warsaw, made a successful tour of the United States. It was significant for improved cultural relations between the United States and Poland and for stimulating the interest of the large Polish American audiences in their heritage.

Prime-Bishop Grochowski of the Polish National Catholic Church began cooperating actively with the Puerto Rican National Catholic Church.

Chester C. Kowal was elected mayor of Buffalo as a Republican.

John Joseph Krol, auxiliary bishop of Cleveland since 1953, was elevated to the archdiocese of Philadelphia. Though there had been ten other Catholic American bishops of Polish ancestry before him, Krol was the first to lead a major American Roman Catholic diocese.

1962

A conference of Protestant churches invited the Polish National Catholic Church to join future talks on church unity.

President Kennedy intervened actively and with some success to prevent Congress from imposing restrictions on aid to and trade with Poland.

Archbishop Krol began three of service as an undersecretary of the Second Vatican Council of the Roman Catholic Church. He took part in the formulation of the Council's statement on the Jews. The Council released a powerful movement for reform which affected the traditional practices of Polish Roman Catholics in the United States. By encouraging Christian church unity and allowing the use of vernacular languages in church services, the Council helped improve relations between Polish Roman and Polish National Catholics.

1963

Benjamin Adamowski, State's Attorney for Cook County, Illinois, challenged Richard Daley seeking re-election as Mayor of Chicago. Daley defeated Adamowski by securing a heavy majority of the vote in the city's Black precincts.

The Polish Courier of Milwaukee ceased publication -- one of several signs in these years of a decline in the Polish language press in the United States.

John Gronouski, Wisconsin Commissioner of Taxation, became Postmaster-General -- the first American of Polish descent to achieve Cabinet level status.

1965

The Immigration Act of 1965 radically altered national immigration policy by basing admissions on such criteria as the needed skills of would-be immigrants and uniting

separated families. The elimination of the old national
quota system was consistent with contemporary civil
rights legislation for it removed the old discrimination
against immigrants from eastern and southern Europe.
Polish emigration to the United States continued in moder-
ate but steady numbers.

John Gronouski retired as Postmaster-General and was
appointed ambassador to Poland, holding the post until
1968.

The American Research Hospital for Children was dedicated in Cracow. Wladek O. Biernacki-Poray, of Mont-
clair, New Jersey, conceived the idea for the hospital
in 1958 and promoted it afterwards. American counterpart funds, private donations and land and services given
by the Polish government helped to make the idea a reality.

1966   American Poles commemorated the millenium of Poland's
nationhood with numerous publications, commemorative
meetings and other forms of recognition. Special notice
by the larger American community took the form of a
Presidential Proclamation -- "Commemoration of
Poland's National and Christian Millenium" -- on May 3rd
and other tokens such as a commemorative stamp. The
celebration was marred by several controversies, notably
the refusal of the Polish government to allow Cardinal
Wyszynski of Warsaw to visit the United States, a heritage
of the changes wrought by World War II and the Cold War.

Martin Luther King and the Southern Christian Leadership
Conference led major demonstrations in Chicago for open
housing. Some of the demonstrations entered Polish
neighborhoods in the city, marking a period of extreme
racial tension.

An important exhibit of art treasures from Poland opened
in Chicago in connection with the nation's millenium.
The following year it was seen in Philadelphia and Ottawa.

The Polish Institute of Arts and Sciences sponsored a
large Congress of Polish American Scholars and Scientists in New York City. It gave witness to the substantial
Polish contribution to the intellectual and scientific life of
of the United States since the 1940's.

About 135,000 people attended the dedication of the Polish Catholic shrine at Doylestown, Pennsylvania. Its erection was due mostly to the leadership of Father Michael Zembruzuski, the Vicar-General of the Pauline Fathers. President Johnson addressed the audience, emphasizing the heritage of freedom for Poles and other minorities in America.

1967   Dial Press published W. S. (Jack) Kuniczak's The 1,000 Hour Day, a popular novel based on the Polish resistance to the German invasion of Poland in 1939. Kuniczak, the son of a Polish army officer in 1939, was a product of the post-war Polish American community.

John L. Waner (Wojnarowski), a liberal Chicago businessman, challenged Richard Daley for mayor of Chicago. He failed badly, not even doing well in the Polish community or among his fellow Republicans.

Archbishop Krol of Philadelphia was named to the Roman Catholic College of Cardinals.

Large-scale racial rioting broke out in many American cities, among them Detroit and Newark -- cities with large Polish American populations.

The Chicago attorney Aloysius Mazewski was elected president of the Polish National Alliance, terminating the twenty-eight year regime of Charles Rozmarek.

The Polish National Catholic Church invited representatives of the Roman Catholic hierarchy to attend its General Synod for the first time.

In an effort to ease the Polish debt of 45 million dollars to the United States, the two countries agreed on a program of English language training in Poland to be financed by the Poles.

The Felician sisters converted Immaculate Conception Junior College in Lodi, New Jersy, into a four year school -- Felician College -- for women.

1968   Reports that the Polish government had adopted policies with anti-Semitic overtones renewed discussion within the United States of Polish-Jewish relations. Cardinal Krol received the Human Relations Award of the National Conference of Christians and Jews.

Residents of the "Polish Hill" community in Pittsburgh rejected participation in the Model Cities program to rejuvenate their neighborhood. They cited an inadequate voice for themselves in planning of the project and the use of the program to advance the interests of outside politicians.

A Detroit Archdiocesan Conference of Polish Priests pledged itself to support the struggle for equal rights for all Americans and called upon their people to join them in the fight. Their action helped to counteract the popular image of Polish attitudes toward other minorities and to maintain interracial harmony in Detroit.

Aloysius Mazewski was elected president of the Polish American Congress, succeeding Charles Rozmarek.

The Democratic party nominated Edmund Muskie as the vice-presidential running-mate of Hubert Humphrey. While the Democrats were defeated narrowly in the national election, Muskie made a strong impression upon voters and professional politicians.

Polish Americans increased their protests against derogatory treatment, exerting direct pressure on such institutions as Columbia Broadcasting System and the University of Notre Dame. They also sought cooperation with Italian American organizations who felt similarly slighted.

1969

The Polish American Congress initiated a major fund drive and program to combat the defamation of Polish Americans. One year later, however, it had reached only ten percent of its goal of half a million dollars.

Jerzy Kosinski, a Polish author now living in the United States, won the 1968 National Book Award for his novel Steps.

The Sisters of the Holy Family of Nazareth announced plans to build a $21.3 million St. Mary of Nazareth health center in Chicago.

Cultural exchanges between Poland and the United States increased significantly as a result of action taken during the year. The State Department announced resumption of a limited official cultural exchange program with Poland. Cardinal Karol Wotyla, Archbishop of Cracow, visited fifteen major cities in the United States. Film producers from Poland visited Polish American communities for the first Polish film about American Poles. The Polish Laboratory Theater, directed by Jerzy Grotowski, made its American debut in New York City. And the Kosciuszko Foundation announced plans for a collegiate junior year of study in Poland in 1970-1971.

The Polish American Congress called together a Convocation of Polish American Scholars at Alliance College to examine the state and the place of the intellectual life among Polish Americans.

Prime-Bishop Leon Grochowski of the Polish National Catholic Church died in Warsaw where he had been attending church conferences.

John Gronouski was appointed Dean of the Lyndon Baines Johnson School of Public Affairs at the University of Texas, Austin.

After a year of meetings Polish and Black leaders in Detroit formed the Black-Polish Conference to bridge the distance between the two communities. Poles made up twenty percent and Blacks forty-three percent of the city's population. Soon afterward, Roman Gribbs (a Pole) defeated a liberal Black candidate to become the first Polish American mayor of Detroit. The campaign was notable for the relative absence of apparent racial conflict.

Buffalo Councilwoman-at-large Mrs. Alfreda Slominski (Republican) lost the city election to Mayor Frank Sedita (Democrat) by the largest margin in the city's history. Here defeat was interpreted as a rejection of a campaign based on the themes of "law and order" and opposition to busing inner-city pupils to previously all-white schools.

Fifteen members of Congress, led by Roman Pucinski (Democrat, Illinois), introduced a bill to establish a series of Ethnic Heritage Studies Centers. Their purpose would have been to develop curriculum and train teachers for studying America's major ethnic groups.

Joseph Yablonski waged a vigorous campaign for the presidency of the United Mine Workers against W. A. (Tony) Boyle. He was defeated, and on New Year's Eve he, his wife and daughter were found murdered in their home. Subsequent investigations led to the overturning of the election on the grounds that union leaders had used illegal campaign tactics.

According to population estimates of the federal government, there were 4,021,000 Americans who were ethnically Polish; 60.2% of them claimed Polish as a mother tongue while 92.6% usually spoke the English language. Polish Americans argued, as they had in the past, that federal census figures underestimated their actual number.

1970

Thomas (Tom) Gola assumed the post of City Controller in Philadelphia -- the first Polish American to hold high office in the city. Gola's career was a good example of upward mobility among Catholic Poles. His father had been a policeman, and he had been a star basketball player for La-Salle College. After a successful career as a professional basketball player, he entered business and then took up politics.

Alliance College began a "Year Abroad Program" at the Jagiellonian University in Cracow in cooperation with the Kosciuszko Foundation.

Attorney Leon Jaworski of Houston, Texas, was named president-elect of the American Bar Association.

After several conferences reaching back to 1969, a Permanent Committee on Polish-Jewish Relations in the United States was formed. The Polish National Alliance and the Anti-Defamation League of B'nai B'rith took the lead in its organization.

Dr. Hilary Koprowski of Philadelphia, a virologist and director of the Wistar Institute, was awarded a grant for $40,000 by the National Multiple Sclerosis Society to investigate "slow virus."

The Task Force on Urban Problems of the United States Catholic Conference focused its attention on issues of ethnic community development.

President Nixon held two meetings at the White House with representatives of Polish American organizations and promised to appoint more qualified Polish Americans to high federal offices. Aloysius Mazewski was named as an alternate member of the United States delegation to the 25th session of the United Nations General Assembly.

Edmund Muskie's nationally televised election eve speech on behalf of Democratic congressional candidates provided a strong impetus to his potential candidacy for the presidential nomination.

1971   Cultural exchanges between Poland and the United States included the American tour of the Poznan Boys Choir; an appeal by a Polish committee to Poles everywhere to assist in rebuilding the Royal Castle in Warsaw (destroyed in the Second World War); and the inauguration of an educational exchange program between Seton Hall University, New Jersey, and the University of Warsaw.

Officials of the Polish American Congress met with federal administrators in Washington in search of fair recognition and equal rights for Polish Americans in all fields of endeavor.

The Polish Daily News of Chicago (Dziennik Chicagoski) ceased publication after eighty-one years. It was one of several Polish language newspapers, among them the New World of New York City, which closed down recently.

The Second Congress of Polish American Scholars and Scientists met in New York City under the sponsorship of the Polish Institute of Arts and Sciences and of the Institute on East Central Europe and the School of International Affairs of Columbia University.

Aloysius Mazewski, on behalf of the Polish American Congress, presented Pope Paul with a memorandum which documented the under-representation of Polish Americans in the American Catholic hierarchy.

Pope Paul participated in the beatification of Father Maximilian Kolbe, martyred in Poland during the Second World War. The presence in Rome of over 750 people organized by the Father Justin Rosary Hour was the largest overseas pilgrimage in the history of Polish America.

At its thirteenth General Synod in Toronto the Polish National Catholic Church elected Bishop T. F. Zielinski as its Prime-Bishop.

Understanding of Polish culture by non-Poles was fostered at a number of levels during the year. The Library of Congress sponsored a successful Polish folklore exhibit organized by Janina Hoskins. The Jurzykowski Foundation of New York City endowed a Chair in Polish Language and Literature at Harvard University; its first occupant was Professor Wiktor Weintraub. The businessman Edward Piszek and the Orchard Lake Schools (St. Mary's College, the Polish Seminary) launched a large, well-publicized and well-financed campaign called "Project Pole." It was designed to educate the American public about Poland and to improve the image and self-image of Polish Americans. Piszek was president and one of the founders in 1946 of Mrs. Paul's Kitchens; he had been involved in a number of public service projects oriented to Polish culture and welfare.

John Cardinal Krol was chosen president of the National Conference of Catholic Bishops and emerged as an important leader of the World Synod of Catholic bishops.

1972

Edmund Muskie officially launched his campaign for the Democratic presidential nomination early in the year. Despite considerable support from party leaders, he was unable to win the support of labor or reform elements in the party. A lack of support in the presidential primaries caused him to withdraw from active campaigning in April.

A United States Senate subcommittee held hearings on a proposal to convert the last residence of Thaddeus Kosciuszko in Philadelphia into a national historic site, further acknowledging Polish participation in American life.

The Polish American Congress joined those forces which sought successfully to continue official funding for Radio Free Europe over the objections of the Senate Foreign Relations Committee.

Congress enacted the Ethnic Heritage Studies bill.

Richard Kolm, a Polish-born sociologist at Catholic University in Washington, D. C., was elected president of the National Coordinating Assembly on Ethnic Studies.

DOCUMENTS

THE POLES AT JAMESTOWN: "FOR THE BENIFITT

OF THE COUNTRY HEREAFTER"

1585-1619

Nearly three centuries separated the Jamestown Poles
from the great Polish migration, but the early settlers
prefigured the later in several important ways. As
anonymous workers mostly, they had a small but solid
part in the beginnings of English America. These are
the principal references to the earliest Polish Americans.

Polish workers played a part in the earliest English thinking about
exploiting the resources of the New World. Richard Hakluyt, an early
promoter of settlement in Virginia, wrote this in 1585: among the "Sorts
of men which are to be passed in this voyage" are "Men skillful in burning
of Soap ashes, and in making of Pitch, and Tarre, and Rozen, to be fetched
out of Prussia and Poland, which are thence to be had for small wages, being there in manner of slaves." Hakluyt's suggestion eventually bore fruit
at Jamestown. During the second year of the colony, about October 1,
1608, John Smith, the President of the Council, noted the arrival of "8.
Dutchmen and Poles." The Dutchmen were Germans.

Smith was sceptical of the company policy which had sent the new
arrivals: "As for the Hiring of the Poles and Dutch, to make pitch and
tarre, glasse, milles, and sope-ashes; that was most necessarie and well.
But to send them and seaventy more without victuall, to worke, was not
so well considered; yet this could not have hurt us, had they bin 200;
though then we were 130 that wanted for our selves. For we had the
Salvages in that Decorum, (their harvest beeing newly gathered) that we
feared not to get victual sufficient, had we bin 500." However, the ship
returned with samples of the products the new men had been sent to
manufacture, and Smith found the Poles to be solid workers and useful
members of the colony. Soon afterwards, while returning from the new
glass-house alone, Smith encountered a local Indian "king," the Werowance
of Paspaheigh, who attacked him physically. "Long they struggled in the
water," recounted Smith, "from whence the king perceiving two of the Poles
upon the sandes, would have fled: but the President held him by the haire
and throat til the Poles came in. Then seeing how pittifully the poore Sal-
vage begged his life, they conducted him prisoner to the fort."

Other Poles followed the first, but they remained nameless except for
one "Robert a Polonian" (Robert Poole) who acted as a trader and inter-
preter and who once stirred up some trouble with the Indians for his personal benefit. In 1619, the year of the House of Burgesses and the beginnings of representative government in the New World, the Records of the

Virginia Company show that the Poles asked for a part in the political process: "Upon some dispute of the Polonians resident in Virginia, it was now agreed (notwithstanding any former order to the contrary) that they shal be enfranchized and made as free as any inhabitant there whatsoever: and because their skill in making pitch and tarre and sope-ashes shall not dye with them, it is agreed that some young men shalbe put unto them to learne their skill and knowlege therein for the benifitt of the Country hereafter."

KAZIMIERZ PULASKI: "I CAME TO HAZARD ALL

FOR THE FREEDOM OF AMERICA"

1779

> Pulaski was a controversial refugee from the political
> troubles of Poland. His last letter to the American
> Congress illustrates many of the qualities of the
> "political" emigrants -- educated, proud, sensitive
> nationalists who looked to America for inspiration and
> support and were often disappointed.

Gentlemen - Every information from the Northward that has reached
me Since my Departure from thence, Strengthens my opinion, indeed --
Convinces me that there is some Malignant Spirit Constantly Casting Such
an impenetrable might before your Eyes, as to render it impossible for you
to See and judge of my Conduct with propriety, and as becomes the Character of Gentlemen in your Exalted Stations.

As an enthusiastic Zeal for the glorious cause which animated America, when I came over, and a contempt of death, first introduced me in your
service, So I flattered myself I should have been happy Enough to acquire
honour and to give Satisfaction; but Such has been my Lot, that nothing
Less than my honour, wich I will never forfeit, retains me in a Service,
wich ill treatment makes me begin to abhor.   Every proceeding respecting
myself has been so thoroughly mortifying, that nothing but the integrity of
my heart, and the fervency of my Zeal Supports me under it.   I am accus-
tomed to Explain myself very freely, and I must do it now.

Is there any one act of mine, Ever Since the battle of Brandywine down
to the present period, the campaign of Charlestown, that has not demon-
strated the most disinterested zeal for the public cause?   I believe the
most profligate of my Enemies Cannot presume to deny it.   Whence comes
it then, that I have so Little Credit among you Gentlemen, that no one
thing wherein I am concerned is done to my Satisfaction? Since the fatal
instant that I undertook to raise my Corps, which I cloathed, Recruited
and Exercised in the space of three mounths time, I have been, and still
am persecuted!   I cannot Express my indignation, when I recollect the
famous chicane by wich I was compelled to appear before a Court like a
criminal.

The delay of Congress to send me against the Enemy was grounded
upon a pretence of misbehaviour of My Corps to several of the inhabitants,
even while certificates from the magistrates wherever my troops were
quartered evidenced the contrary.   Altho my Corps behaved with firmness
at Little Egg Harbour, and Several officers and soldiers fell or were
wounded, their only reward was slander.   My often repeated request to have
the accounts of the Corps settled while I was present has been rejected;
and, after a whole years delay, when Several officers whose presence was
necessary to prove those accounts, were either killed or gone out of the

Service it is pretended that they Shall be Settled with the Greatest Exactness; Lieut. Col. Bose is killed, Major Monfort, and Capt. Caillivy have quited the Service and gone to Europe: Col. Kowaths is killed and Lieut. Seydling prisoner with the Ennemy, each of those Gentlemen were entrusted with some department. You must remember that my request to settle those accounts while it Could be done with ease and while those Gentlemen were present, was repeated a thousand times; therefore if there is any irregularity in the vouchers, it cannot be imputed to me or to Capt. Baldeski; and those who occasioned the Delay ought to be answerable for the whole. Besides the sum, wich Seems so extravagant to you, is but a mere triffle to the States; indeed to me for tho I do not abound in Riches yet it is not impossible for myself to repay the whole expenses of my Legion -- the Value of paper money at present is 20. for 1 in coin, so that if I apply 30,000 Livres towards it, that will produce a sum of 600,000 in paper money at Least four times the amount of the Expense that are disputed and with wich I am upbraided. Give me Leave Gentlemen to be plain with you. You are, in this case, Rather ungenerous; and here are foreigners to whom that attention has not been pay'd wich they had just Grounds to Expect from you. You cannot be ignorant, that I have spent Considerably more than the Sum in question, of my own, for the pleasure of advancing your cause, you must be sensible also that I (did not) Come to America destitute of Resources, to be a burthen on you. That I have a Letter of Credit on Mr. Moris; and that I was known by almost Every foreigner of Character.

I have lately Received Letter from my Family advising, that they dispatched 100,000 Livres in hard money to me, Should it fortunately come Safe, the pleasure to me will be truly great to repay you to the utmost farthing, the whole charge of my Legion. Change then your opinion of one foreigner, who from his intrance into your Service, has never the cause to be pleased; who, in Europe, is by Rank superior to all that are in your Service; who certainly is not inferior in Zeal and Capacity and who perhaps, may have been considered as one who came to beg your favour. Be more just, Gentlemen, and Know that as I could not Submit to Stoop before the Sovereigns of Europe, So I came to hazard all the freedom of America, and desirous of passing the rest of my life in a Country truly free and before settling as a Citizen, to fight for Liberty; but perceiving that endeavors are used to disgart me against Such a motive, and to regard it as phantom, I am inclined to believe that enthusiasm for Liberty is not the predominant Virtue in America at this time. I have been informed, that the board of war instead of detaining or punishing deserters from my Legion, have discharged them from the Service; can this be called a proper Conduct towards men who rob the State of the bounty and other wise? I have also been informed that one man hearing of this Generosity and who had Stolen a horse to desert with, apply to them, was not only favoured in Like manner: but Even presented with the Horse. The officers who would have done their duty in maryland imposed a penalty of 100 upon any man who should inlisted in my Corps. Capt. Bedkin who was Left, with a detachment of Light horse, to colect men remaining behind sick or on furlough with horses belonging to the Legion, and enthrusted with the sum of 5000 dollars for the recruiting Service has found protection with the Same board, who have rendered him independent altho he has failed in the Duty of an honest man. What does all this indicate? Has it not the appearance of an insidious design of disaffected persons to urge me to quit the Service in disgust, without minding the justice of their proceedings. Such a person I denounce to your tribunal as perturbators of the Peoples welfare in the military Line.

It is my disposition to Speak so as to be perfectly understood. I honour you without baseness, flattery is noxious in private as well as public bodies; it is the vice of those base animals who endeavour to persecute and injure me.

I was present when General Lincoln received an Express with a Letter mentioning Capt. Baldeski's detention and the order for appointing another paymaster with office I believe is not very necessary, the few men we have left might be pay'd by the General paymaster of the Army, and there will be no further confusion in the Details. Moreover, it seems that the destruction of the Corps is intended wich will be eased performed.

The Campaign is at hand, perhaps I may still (have) an occasion of showing that I am a friend to the cause without being happy enough to please some ind . . .

I have the honour to be Gentlemen with Respect your most humble and obedient Servant. C. Pulaski. Charlestown August the 19th, 1779.

KOSCIUSZKO'S WILL: "TO MAKE THEMSELVES HAPPY AS POSSIBLE"

1797

Thaddeus Kosciuszko was the most important of the hundreds of Polish exiles who settled for all or part of their lives in the United States. His will, made just prior to his leaving America for the second time, is an example of the libertarian and humanitarian strain among the early Polish exiles. What follows is the first draft of a will which Jefferson rewrote and which was later superseded.

I beg Mr. Jefferson that in case I should die without will or testament he should bye out of my money so many Negroes and free them, that the restant Sum should be Sufficient to give them education and provide for their maintenance. That is to say each should know before, the duty of a Cytyzen in the free Government, that he must defend his Country against foreign as well internal Enemis who would wish to change the Constitution for the vorst to inslave them by degree afterwards, to have good and human heart sensible for the sufferings of others, each must be maried and have 100 ackres of land, wyth instruments, Cattle for tillage and know how to manage and Gouvern it as well to know how behave to neybourghs, always wyth kindness and ready to help them- to them selves frugal, to their Children give good education I mean as to the heart, and the duty to ther Country, in gratitude to me to make themselves happy as possible. T Kosciuszko.

REFUGEES OF THE REVOLUTION OF 1830: "WE WISH TO PLANT IN THESE UNITED STATES A SECOND POLAND"

1834

Polish immigrants, like many others, often had romantic visions of re-establishing their old homeland in the United States. The proposal of the 1834 band of exiles led to a Congressional grant of land in Illinois but was abondoned ultimately.

Memorial to the representatives of the people of the United States of America in Congress assembled:

The undersigned Poles, selected by the 235 placed on the hospitable shores of these United States by the orders of the emperor of Austria, venture to address your august body for such relief as men placed in our peculiar situation may lay claim to.

As long as we had a country that we could call our own, we resolutely fought for her independence, until the overwhelming power of Russia forced us to take refuge in the Austrian and Prussian provinces, asking only for a free passage into France. In the month of April last the Austrian government having promised us liberty and protection, suddenly, and without notice, placed us in confinement in the city of Brunn, in Moravia, answering our protests with assurances that, when assembled, we would be sent to France. After three months' confinement, the Austrian government gave us the choice of either returning to Russia or of embarking for the United States, with the government of which an arrangement had been made for our protection and support. As lovers of freedom and of free institutions, we accepted the alternative of living among a free people; although in so doing we had to give up all hopes of the land of our love, of our habits, of our laws, and our language. Arrived at Trieste, we were there confined for three months, until, finally we were embarked on board of two Austrian frigates and after a navigation of four months and ten days, landed at New York, in these United States, where we now find ourselves placed in the most critical situation, being ignorant alike of the language and of the customs of the country, and destitute of everything but the means of a few days' support.

Although pilgrims in a foreign land, with nothing but the sad recollections of the past, and hopes for the future, we wish to live a life of active industry and become useful to the country of our adoption. Since Providence in its inscrutable wisdom has deprived us of the land of our birth, we wish to plant in these United States a second Poland, where our countrymen, the still unconquered sons of adversity, may congregate and prosper.

With these views, we respectfully solicit your august body a grant of land under such provisions as will enable us to live by our industry, to rally round us such of our countrymen as may visit these shores, and become of use and of service to the people of these United States, and for such other aid and assistance as may seem meet. And your petitioners, as in duty bound, will ever pray.

New York, April 9, 1834.

Lew. Banczakiewicz, Mart. Rosienkiewicz, Dr. Char. Kraitsir, John Rychlicki, Fel. Gronczewski, Jos. Kosowski, John Hiz, Lew. Jezykowicz, Adalb. Konarzewski.

GASPARD TOCHMAN: "TO SAVE THE PRINCIPLES WHICH UNDERLIE

THE CONSTITUTION OF THE UNITED STATES"

1861

When the American Civil War broke out most of the Polish exile community identified its cause with the Union and the gradual extinction of slavery. Gaspard Tochman, however, had assimilated the contemporary Southern opinion of the Union and of American race relations. His letter to the Polish Democratic Societies abroad summarizes his views.

To the Polish Democratic Societies, in France and England.

CITIZENS: -- Your joint resolutions (bearing dates "Paris -- France, August 26th, 1861," and "London -- England, August 27th, 1861,") inquiring into "my motives and policy of deviating from the Consitution of the United States of North America, which I swore to support," and censuring me for "enlisting into the service of, and raising a Brigade of troops for, the States which seceded from, and are waging war against said United States" -- have reached me last week in the City of Nashville, State of Tennesee.

I assert that, in tendering my services to the Confederate States, I have fulfilled the requirements of the Constitution of the United States "which I swore to support," and consequently that, no other "motives and policy" but the duty of sustaining those which guided the framers of that Constitution and are embodied in it, have induced me to side with the Confederate States in this most unnatural and deplorable war: Finally, I assert that, the obligation -- evolving from the dictates of natural law -- to preserve our species in its purity from deterioration; the unbiassed humanity controlled by right reason; and, the allegiance due to the reserved sovereignties of the States, constituting federal union, underlie that Constitution, -- and my conduct will be found consistent, in every respect, with all these principles.

. . . .

From the early period of European settlements -- there existed, on the original domain of the United States, a society formed of two races of our species, the white, (Caucasion race) free and dominant -- and the black, (African race,) subjected to the former, slave or bound to service. The aborigines, (native Indians,) have never made a component part of that society. The white and black races only constituted and represented it, in twelve out of thirteen then existing communities: all thirteen, being entirely independent one of the other -- governed themselves internally by their own laws, and local institutions -- enacted or adapted by the dominant whole race -- yet, defining social duties and rights of both, white and black

49

races respectively, and extending and securing the legal protection of life equally to each of them. The external policy of these thirteen colonies centred in the government of the British empire of which they made, then, a component part. The attempt of that government to extend its interference in the internal affairs of the colonies, and to enlarge the external policy -- provoked that revolution which achieved their independence. That revolution, however, left unaltered and unscathed their corporate internal-life, their social and political organizations, and their fibres -- the local laws, institutions, customs, and civil and political rights; except only so far as the memorable Declaration of Independence changed them from dependent colonies to independent States -- united together by that Declaration, in the manner and for the purposes defined by the subsequent Act of Confederation, which created and established their FIRST federal government. It is submitted, that Declaration of Independence asserts the people's right to self-government, and also their right to change their governments and create new, whenever the old cease to answer the ends for which they had been established; and, the Act of Confederation (the first fundamental law of the new-born federal Republic,) consonant with that assertion in the Declaration of Independence, expressly reserves to each State "its sovereignty, freedom, and independence." After the European powers, including Great Britain, had acknowleged the independence of so constituted and organised federal body politic -- under the name of the United States of North America, its people finding their first government inadequate for the task, ordained its reconstruction, and established a new federal government defined in the famous fundamental law -- the Constitution of the United States. But this Constitution was not enacted and ratified by the collective concurrence of the people of the United States, acting in the aggregate capacity. Its draught or delineation, its adoption and ratification, were wrought out by individual nations of each State; each acting in its sovereign capacity -- by Delegates, Conventions and Legislatures; each had but one vote in the ratification -- without regard to the disparity of the States as to their territorial extents and populations. The States, then, as sovereigns -- representing their people, consistently with the principles of the original federal Union, established and inaugurated this new federal government. It possessed only certain delegated powers, which relate chiefly to the external policy, and such internal as is aggregate in its nature, to the rights arising under the Constitution, the laws enacted under its authority, the treaties with foreign nations, and such other as are specifically enumerated in that Constitution. The powers which are vital in this governmental fabric -- relating to the internal policy, social institutions, civil and political rights of citizens, such as are bearing upon their liberty, independence, life and property of every kind, remained (as they were before the adoption of the Constitution) vested in the States -- together with all other powers not delegated to the federal government specifically -- which are expressly reserved to the States. The domestic local institutions, relating to the African race, have however, been modified -- by authorising Congress to supress their importation from abroad -- which was done accordingly in 1808; and those Africans who make here a part of domestic society, have been elevated -- by designation in the Constitution, as "persons bound to service" -- "persons held to labour" instead of "slaves" -- and by its allowing to the States where such "persons" exist, the representation -- vote of three fifths of their number -- to wit: three votes for each five "persons bound to service" or Africans. A wise and humane elevation of that race of men, -- which by a logical consequence makes their labour the property of its owner, secures and protects it Constitutionally as such, and yet acknowleges them to be men of inferior race -- consistently with the dictates of the law of their nature -- whereby it pleased Providence, to segregate them from the homogeneous society of the Caucasian race, by the inborn differences in their organism and its properties, which no human law can alter. I have touched this subject not to argue it with you, at this time, but solely to show that "persons bound to service" here, are not the slaves of Socrates; nor are they slaves of Rome and other ancient and modern nations -- made slaves by the human laws of conquest, or restraints of the developments of intellectual capacities. The framers of the Constitution of the United States -- as well as the original founders of Colonies, had to mould here rules for society, not upon the abstract theories; but conformably to the innate properties and organisms of two races of men, naturally differing. They did so with practical wisdom -- and philanthropy guided by right reason -- to preserve our own race from amalgamation, which the law of nature punishes with deterioration and extinction of the superior race, in the gradually weakening progeny of mulattoes. That the elimination of the black's blood is inconsistent with the nature, and ends in the deterioration and such extinction of the superior race, has been practically and scientifically proved. [Cites sources.]

When I contemplate the miseries of amalgamations of inferior races with the superior of our species -- which their social and political equality not adjusted to the requirements of the inherent properties in their organisms, has produced in Mexico and the States of South America: when I look at, and consider the results of unrestrained to the natural effects of those properties, French and English emancipations, in the West Indies; and then cast my unbiassed rational reflection on the condition of "persons bound to service" under the protective American philanthropy, wrought out by the practical and scientific experience and embodied in their Constitution of the United States; opposed as I have always been to slavery, in Europe, I cannot help admiring the wisdom of that Constitution, in settling here this question in the way and manner it has done it, as co-equal with that of the system of its complicated-government, to prevent the centralization of political power. The States -- like the planets revolving around the sun -- all equal as to their beings, though different in sizes and inherent components; each independent of the other, not blended in the federal government, and yet by its delegated and their original residuary powers, causing mutual attractions and repulsions, -- balancing, keeping in the appropriate orbits, and vivifying each other, by unseen forces; -- present, indeed, to the beholder the most perfect fabric of a free and effective federal, democratic government. [He summarizes the abolition and free soil movements, concluding that their success and the uncompromising policy of the Lincoln administration finally forced the slaves states to secede.]

. . . . These are the facts which history has recorded on the wall of destiny. I submit them to you for consideration -- without comments -- in support of the assertions which I set forth at the outset of this answer. I only add, that were I a citizen of any of the Northern States which effected this result, most injurious and terrible to mankind and its democracy, I would side in this struggle with the Southern Confederacy; because, having taken the oath of naturalization to support the Constitution of the United States, I could not conscientiously, join the crusade against the States which adhere to its principles. And besides, the Union upheld by the bayonets of the Northern section, would be as much Federal Constitutional Union as is our beloved Poland a State free and independent under the bayonets of Russia. It would become a theatre of successive revolts for many generations, as Poland is now; and might become another Human,* or perhaps Hayti. Washington, Lafayette, Kosciusko, Pulaski, DeKalb, and their illustrious associates, had not fought for such an Union; and I, their humble worshipper, with my eyes opened and judgment clear on the subject, would never do it. To save the principles which underlie the Constitution of the United States, when the Union could not have been saved, is now, I believe, the duty of all the friends of freedom and mankind; for, when these principles are saved, they will develop and expand as all things in nature do when the seed is saved. The Confederate States, in this conflict, uphold precisely this law of nature; they are fighting to save those principles from perishing in the sectional centralism . . . .

*The rebellion of serfs, instigated and caused by the Government of Russia, before Poland fell, commenced in the District of Human, and is known in the History of Poland by that name.

THE CHURCH OF ST. STANISLAUS KOSTKA: "WHEREVER THERE IS A PRIEST, A CHURCH, WHEREVER A PARISH IS BEING CREATED, THERE POLISH LIFE GROWS VIGOROUSLY"

1907

Without a clear plan or intellectual formulation, the Polish peasants who migrated to the farms and factories of the United States in the third quarter of the nineteenth century worked their way through to a new small community -- an extended parish based somewhat on the Old World village and eventually satisfying most of the non-job needs of its members. This history of the beginnings of the largest Polish parish in America is drawn from its fiftieth anniversary album.

Not much information has been preserved about the first beginnings of the parish of St. Stanislaus Kostka in Chicago . . . . In 1864 . . . about 30 families belonged to the Polish settlement in Chicago and these organized the first Polish association in this city with the name, Society of Fraternal Help, and under the patronage of St. Stanislaus Kostka. Its organizers were Anton Smarzewski-Schermann (the first permanent Polish settler in Chicago), Peter Kiolbassa, the well-known leader of the Polonia[1] of Chicago, respected and esteemed by the whole city (he came from Silesia), John Niemczewski, John Arkuszewski and Paul Kurr . . . . Alas, ...after a short existence the society fell . . . .

In 1864 after the strenuous efforts of Peter Kiolbassa and after many requests from the Polish settlers in Chicago, Father Leopold Moczygemba arrived. He had been traveling as a missionary in Texas and other southern States, and came only to hear the Easter confessions of the Poles. But his stay became memorable and important, because he was the first Polish priest who had come to his fellow-citizens in Chicago with religious services.

The Polish colony received Father Moczygemba with vivid joy and in a really elevated spirit. The stay of this pastor in the Chicago settlement revived wonderfully the desire for a stable and permanent organization. For it is a well-known and certain thing that . . . wherever there is a priest, a church, wherever a parish is being created, there Polish life grows vigorously, there our number multiplies, for from all sides people come willingly, feeling better among their own and with their own, feeling safer under the protective wings of the parish and with their own shepherd, who here in a foreign land is not only a representative of his brothers before the altar of the Lord but leads and represents them in all worldly affairs. . . is in the whole sense of this word, a social and national worker.

Thus in our settlement, which was continually growing because of the influx of immigrants, in the beginning of 1866 the idea was taken up of calling to life again the Society of St. Stanislaus . . . . Indeed, it was revived so thoroughly that it grew soon to be quite important and has remained up to now the first permanent union of the Poles in our city . . . . The constitution of the society was accepted June 1st, 1866. It was printed in Paris. The first officers of the association were . . . .

After the existence of the Society of St. Stanislaus and its further development were assured, the spirit of organization, once aroused in our settlement, did not rest. And they began to think about founding a Polish parish in Chicago. In the beginning . . . there was no Polish priest and the divine service was performed for the Poles in turn by the rector of the Czech parish, Father Molitor, and by the Jesuit, Father Szulak . . . . The time about which we are speaking was the year 1867. The settlement counted about 150 families mostly from Silesia when they finally began to think about buying land for a church of their own . . . . Four lots were bought at the corner of Noble and Bradley Streets . . . for $1,700. The place chosen then was quite isolated . . . , but since some decision had to be taken in order to establish at last the much desired parish . . . the construction of the church was started in September, 1869 . . . . The church was under the patronage of St. Stanislaus Kostka, built of wood. The first floor was designed for school rooms and had a hall for meetings. On the second floor was the church. The entire cost of the building was $6,885 . . . .

Father Joseph Juszkiewicz was appointed the first rector of the parish. . . . In 1870 Father Adolf Bakanowski from the Order of the Resurrection of Our Lord came to Chicago . . . . The growth of the parish promised to be quite good. Unhappily, for various reasons dissatisfaction and misunderstandings arose until finally the parish stood in open opposition to its rector, Father Juszkiewicz . . . . The parishioners reproached the priest with insufficient care for the parish, which was undeveloped and poor, and finally went to Father Bakanowski eagerly petitioning him to become their rector instead of Father Juszkiewicz. Father Bakanowski refused, explaining that he did not belong to the diocese, that he was dependent upon his Order and was on the way to Rome. In order to show that he had no personal interest in the whole affair and not t be suspected of intriguing between the quarrelling parties he moved to the other end of the city . . . .

Meanwhile among the Polonia disorders continued and finally the excitement reached a point where it nearly ended fatally. One night 6 masked men rang the door-bell of Father Juszkiewicz and when he opened the door beat him severely, threatening him with death if he did not leave the parish. An inquiry began, but nothing certain could be discovered. Finally Father Juszkiewicz left the parish, and Bishop Foley appealed to Father Bakanowski and appointed him rector of the parish, at the same time informing the Superior of the Order of Resurrectionists, Father Kajsiewicz in Rome . . . .

The work in the parish of St. Stanislaus was very tiring for Father Bakanowski; it was much harder here than the missionary work in Texas, where the difficulties of geographical conditions and climate were the only ones, whereas in Chicago it was necessary to struggle with a complex of hostile social elements, parties absorbed in politics, headed mostly by men who were not worth much and who belonged to various American secret societies -- they say even to Masonic lodges. To those pseudo-progressives the calm and noiseless domination of the Catholic Church and religious practices were undesirable. Therefore they made continual trouble and placed obstacles in the way of every positive initiative . . . . Meanwhile news came from the Order of Resurrectionists that this Order took the Chicago mission under its protection and appointed Father Bakanowski its head. Father J. Wollowski was designated as his assistant because the Polish colony was growing very rapidly both with regard to the number of the population and with regard to the territory inhabited by the Poles . . . .

June 18, 1871, the church was very solemnly consecrated. The act of consecration was performed by Bishop Foley of the Chicago diocese, and several fraternities and associations from neighboring parishes of other nationalities took part in this Polish celebration. The property of the new church was deeded to the Bishop in trust for the Order of Resurrectionists. The celebration was concluded by a splendid and, for that time, large parade through the streets of the city in which 2,200 persons took part in orderly lines with standards under the leadership of 11 marshals on horseback. Eight non-Polish associations participated in this parade and some of these had to come 5 miles, a proof how at that time people were interested in every new religious center . . . .

After the great fire of 1871 the conditions in Chicago were greatly changed in every respect. These changes were for the better. The city began to be feverishly rebuilt. In all economical fields intense activity manifested itself; there was much work, a great demand for workers, and a large influx of immigrants. Many Poles came during this period to our city, the greatest number to settle in the north-western part of the town in the neighborhood of the parish of St. Stanislaus. Consequently, the parish grew very much in a short time and new difficulties appeared, for the church became too small to hold the parishioners. This trouble was discussed for a long time at meetings of the parish council. There were many understandings and misunderstandings. Some wanted to rebuild or extend the church, others favored the establishment of a new parish in the neighborhood. Finally, the matter was left in the hands of the two main associations, the older Society of St. Stanislaus and the younger Society of St. Joseph. After a long discussion, which did not always progress peaceably, the foundation of a new parish and the construction of another church was decided. In this way the parish under the patronage of the Holy Trinity came to be founded . . . .[2]   In the same year 21 acres of land were bought for a Polish and Czechish cemetery in Nilles, Ill. . . .

In 1873 Father Bakanowski went to Rome . . . and in 1874 Father Vincent Michael Barzynski, of the Resurrectionists, the greatest and most prominent leader of the American Polonia, an incomparable organizer, was appointed rector of the parish of St. Stanislaus . . . . Among the first acts of Father Barzynski in our parish was the building of a rectory at the cost of $1,500. The same year he entrusted the parochial school to the sisters of the Order of Notre Dame of Milwaukee, Wis. Since that time this Order has conducted our school for many years and the sisters by their thorough and highly competent pedagogical work have made this school one of the best, largest, and most important Polish schools in America. We must further mention as a happening of particular importance, not only for the parish itself but for the whole American Polonia, the organization of a general Polish meeting or diet in October, 1874, in our Stanislawowo [community surrounding the church of St. Stanislaus -- usual way of naming Polish American communities] . To this diet came 12 Polish priests and a number of delegates sent by various Polish parishes. The chief initiator of this diet and of the plans which it formed was Father Barzynski. He propagated the idea of a general Polish organization [which later developed under the name of] . . . . The Polish Roman Catholic Union.

About this time a new Polish parish was organized in the southern part of the city under the patronage of St. Wojciech [Adalbert]--the present Wojciechowo. Father Barzynski rendered meritorious services in connection with this work, for he did not by any means limit his activity to his own parish, but extended it soon over the whole local Polonia and even more distant Polish parishes within a wide radius, organizing settlements, colonies, parishes in settlements and colonies, caring for the spiritual needs of his fellow-citizens, like a real good elder-brother of his brethren . . . .

In 1875 land was bought for a new church, for the old one had long ago proved insufficient. Lots were bought between Bradley and Ingraham Streets for $11,500 and on this place arose, thanks to the intense personal efforts of Father Barzynski, the present splendid church of St. Stanislaus, one of the most beautiful and largest churches in Chicago . . . . In 1878 a new rectory was built near the church, . . . in 1879 a house for the sisters working in the parochial school . . . . The value of the parochial real estate had already reached the sum of $100,000 -- very high for those times. . . . We must mention the foundation in 1882, on the initiative of Father John Radziejewski and with the help of Father Barzynski, of a new Polish parish in South Chicago under the patronage of the Immaculate Conception of the Holiest Virgin Mary, for the Poles in this district of the city were too far distant from the other Polish parishes and were thus deprived of the possibility of frequenting a Polish church . . . . In 1883 the old church building was repaired and turned into a school-building, because the old school was already over-crowded. . . . In 1884 we find a new proof of the industry and wide interests of Father Barzynski. It is a well-known and well remembered fact that under the influence of Father Barzynski a whole series of new parishes was organized in the city and its environs. In the year mentioned the parish of St. Jozafat was founded, more than a mile to the north of the parish of St. Stanislaus . . . . In the same year the church was beautifully painted inside under the supervision and according to the plans of the prominent Polish painter Thaddeus Zukotynski. Finally, on the initiative of Stanislawowo, land was bought for the church of a new parish organized under the patronage of St. Jadwiga . . . .

In 1889 a new school was built, an enormous four-story building raised at the cost of $95,000 . . . . The new building contained 16 schoolrooms, 4 halls for meetings, and an enormous hall with a stage containing 4,000 seats, the second largest in the city, designed for theatrical performances, national celebrations and other public meetings . . . . In 1890 the parish was visited by the General Superior of the Order of Resurrectionists, Father Valerian Przewlocki, who remained among us for a few months . . . . The year is also memorable because during it higher courses for the students of our parochial schools were commenced which became the nucleus of the College of St. Stanislaus, a well-known institution which for 25 years has worked honorably in the field of Polish education in America. This institution has become a real alma mater of a large number of our local workers, is the hotbed of our own Polish American intellectual class. The initiative of these courses was due again to the father and guardian of the Polonia of Chicago, Father Barzynski, in cooperation with Father General Przewlocki . . . . in 1896 a two weeks' revival under the leadership of the Jesuits took place in our parish. This revival brought good fruit and contributed in a considerable measure to the progress of religious spirit and the improvement of mores . . . . The year 1899 covered the parish of St. Stanislaus with deep mourning which spread like a pall over the whole Polonia of Chicago and even over all the Polish emigrants in America. Father Vincent Barzynski died. . . . His funeral took place on May 5, with an enormous attendance of clergy, of many prominent personalities and of a numberless crowd of people. The funeral procession was a great manifestation, an homage of grateful fellow countrymen to the great merits of the prominent priest-patriot . . . . In 1903 in connection with the parochial school free lectures were established for young people who had finished their studies, based on the model of the People's Universities. Every Sunday after the divine service several hundred young people came to these lectures. The subjects were Polish literature, Polish history, natural sciences, rights and duties of citizens, etc. The lecturers were priests and laymen . . . .

In 1906 the large parochial school, the pride of the parish, burned down . . . . On the initiative of the rector, Father Gordon, a new building was immediately begun. Our parish during this very difficult year received help from all sides . . . . Among others, the action of the association under the name The Polish Theater is worth remembering. This association organized for the benefit of the school a splendid Polish performance in the Auditorium, the largest theatrical hall in Chicago . . . . The building of the new parochial school is one of the largest of its kind and constructed in accordance with the latest demands of architectural technique. It cost $250,000 . . . . In 1908 a new building containing the parish hall was solemnly dedicated . . . . This hall, beautifully decorated and containing 1,000 seats, has become rapidly the center of the Polish theatrical activities in Chicago . . . . On May 10th of the same year occurred the splendid celebration in connection with the dedication of the school, made memorable by the visit of the Vice-President of the United States, Mr. Charles Fairbanks. There had probably never yet been in our district or even in all Polish Chicago an equally imposing manifestation . . . . A special reception committee appointed by Father Gordon received the Vice-President at the station . . . . The celebration began with an enormous parade of Polish associations. At least 8,000 persons participated in the parade and more than 20,000 followed it. . . . Later Archbishop Quigley, assisted by numerous clergy, performed the act of consecrating the new buildings while the associations paraded before the tribune of the Vice-President with shouts and waving standards . . . . Everything manifested to the Vice-President the sincere loyalty of our people to the United States which has given them welfare and protection of their liberty. At the same time the celebration showed to the representative of the United States government and to the whole American society the power of the Polish element in this city and in the whole country. It was an imposing presentation of the results of our laborious progress . . . . Afterwards the rector showed to his guest all the school-rooms, where Mr. Fairbanks saw our children the future citizens of this country, and in case of need sincere defenders of the starry flag. They visited 50 schoolrooms in which nearly 4,000 children were being educated . . . . Mr. Fairbanks talked with the children. In a few classes the children sang Polish and American hymns. . . . Finally, a banquet for more than 400 persons was given by the Citizens' Club of Thaddeus Kosciuszko . . . .

In the summer of the same year the American Poles obtained finally, after many years of strenuous efforts, the first realization of their sup-plices preces to the Vatican. Our fellow-countryman, Father Paul Rhode, was appointed Assistant-Bishop of the diocese of Chicago . . . . Everybody remembers those enormous demonstrations in the city of Chicago -- the attendance of the Polish clergy from the whole of the United States more numerous than ever, that glorious parade through the city with chariots, standards, musical bands and torches. It was the largest parade the Poles of Chicago had ever arranged and one of the largest the city had ever seen. As the oldest and largest parish, St. Stanislaus took a very prominent part in these manifestations . . . . We must mention that Reverend Bishop Rhode was a pupil of our parish school . . . .

In 1909 there came to Chicago Archbishop Joseph Weber, who was appointed Superior of the Resurrectionists in America . . . . In 1912, the first summer course was opened for the teaching nuns, on the initiative of Bishop Rhode. . . . In 1914 in connection with our parish school a two year commercial course was founded on the model of the American business college, in order to facilitate for our youth the commercial education which is so necessary in this country.

[1]"Polonia" is a name frequently applied to the totality of Poles in America, or to any local community of Poles in this country.

[2]The author does not present this matter very fully because the clergy of the parish of St. Stanislaus and the Order of Resurrectionists were violently opposed to the foundation of the new parish and the latter was an act of secession performed by the Society of St. Joseph and successful only because of an appeal directly to the Pope.

COMMUNITY THEATER: "THE GREAT SCHOOL OF

NATIONAL VIRTUES AND THE HIGHER EMOTIONS"

1907

Drawn also from St. Stanislaus Kostka's fiftieth anniversary album, this document illustrates the comprehensiveness of the parish organization for the Polish immigrant.

The founder of the Dramatic Circle in the parish of St. Stanislaus was Father Vincent Barzynski of sainted memory. This happened in the following way. The patriotic organization then existing which had the aim of unifying all the associations in the parish for more efficient patriotic work arranged in 1891 a splendid 3 days' celebration of the hundredth anniversary of the Constitution of May 3 in connection with the great national meeting in the former enormous hall of St. Stanislaus. During this manifestation a performance of the Defence of Czestochowa, an episode from "The Deluge" of Sienkiewicz arranged for the theater by Szczesny Zahajkiewicz, was given. Volunteers from choirs and parochial associations were called to perform the particular roles and the result was a great success . . . . This solemn opportunity gave birth to the Dramatic Circle, with the participation of the following amateurs [34 persons mentioned] . . . . The first administration was composed as follows . . . [13 names given] . The purpose of the Circle was to spread the spirit of Polonism among the youth and the means was weekly evenings and theatrical representations in the maternal language.

The first great performance of the Circle after its formal establishment was on October 18, 1891, when for the first time the play of Zahajkiewicz, The Children of Israel, was given. The following year an unusual honor befell the Dramatic Circle. The most famous Polish dramatic artist and one of the foremost stars of the world's theater, Helena Modrzejewska Modjeska appeared twice on our stage together with the amateurs of the Dramatic Circle. The first time she played the role of Kogucina in the Peasant Aristocrats of Anczyc. The second time she played the role of Queen Jadwiga in a dramatic presentation under the same title written especially for Modrzejewska by Zahajkiewicz and dedicated to her . . . . The income from the first performance was offered by the artist to the Polish orphanage, that from the second to the parochial library . . . . Nearly 6,000 persons attended the performance. The enormous hall proved too small and many people had to resign the pleasure of admiring her . . . .

Outside of the Dramatic Circle the Theater of Stanislawowo soon became the field of other activities and efforts to develop among our public better taste and higher theatrical judgment. In this respect the above mentioned S. Zahajkiewicz merited great recognition. He was the first theatrical manager in our Polonia. He trained the actors, wrote popular and Biblical plays especially appreciated by the local public, and thus aroused interest in the stage.   After him Karol Wachtel introduced on the stage the serious Polish repertoire and made several attempts to organize a permanent Polish theater in Chicago -- a stage-manager and actor who received his artistic education in the fatherland.   He is above the amateur level and has managed the artistic side of the theatrical performances of various societies of Stanislawowo.   Under his leadership a number of classical Polish dramas have been given on the stage of Stanislawowo . . . .

The theater of Stanislawowo is now the best Polish theater in Chicago and probably even in all American Polonia.   It has therefore a good chance of becoming a permanent Polish theater, the great school of national virtues and the higher emotions.

THE FRATERNAL ASSOCIATION: "FOR MUTUAL

MORAL AND MATERIAL ASSISTANCE"

1900-1907

The heart of parish society was the small mutual aid society, meeting the need for the company of others, sustaining the moral discipline of the community and assisting with the extraordinary expense of a satisfactory funeral. Few things mattered or cost so much in life as the leaving of it. United, these societies provided the substance of the national fraternals who led Polish Americans into the larger American society. This example is also taken from the fiftieth anniversary album of St. Stanislaus Kostka in Chicago.

The Association of Polish Women [under the patronage] of God's Mother of Czestochowa (No. 53 of the Polish Roman Catholic Union) was organized on January 29th, 1900, in the parish of St. Stanislaus Kostka by Father John Kasprzycki who was then curate of this parish. The first administration of the Association was composed of the following members [11 names] . . . .

Its aim is to have the Polish women hold to the principles of the Roman Catholic faith and national traditions, for mutual moral and material assistance. By moral assistance we understand developing and promoting friendship, unity and real sisterly love, and spreading education in the Christian and national spirit. By material assistance we understand paying to the remaining family after the death of a member the sum for which she was insured. The Association holds meetings the second Sunday of every month. The Association of Polish Women... admits only members of Polish nationality from 14 to 45 years of age, who must have the proper qualifications required by the constitutions of the Union and of the Association. The Association remains under the supervision of the Most Reverend Archbishop and under the control of the local curate or of his vicar in religious and moral matters.

[Besides the insurance in the Union.] . . . In case of the death of a member who had belonged to the Association for 6 months, the latter pays to the heir or heirs $75.00 for funeral expenses. At the funeral of a member who had not fallen behind in her payments the Association orders a Holy Mass for her soul, appears in corpore at the divine service, hires two coaches or one automobile and buys flowers worth $10.00. The members are obliged to go to confession and to Holy Communion twice a year, on the solemn feast of the Immaculate Conception of the Holiest Virgin Mary and during Easter time, as appointed by the Priest curate. The election of officers is performed in accordance with the constitution of the Polish Roman Catholic Union. The guardians of the treasury audit it every three months. The treasurer, the financial secretary and the guardians of the treasury must deposit bonds.

There is no doubt that the Association of Polish Women of God's Mother of Czestochowa has noble and elevated aims, dries the tears of orphans, obliges itself to nurse and to assist the sick, and to spread the Catholic principles, the commands of love of God and our neighbor. All the activities at meetings are carried on in Polish. To the praise of our sisters it must be also said that at their meetings reign perfect order, concord and sisterly love. No one can reproach the Association of Polish Women . . . for any injustice nor for the violation of the constitution of the Association itself or of the Union.

The Association during the relatively short period of its existence has given some theatrical representations for philanthropic aims, organized excursions for the benefit of the new parish school, made a contribution to the College of St. Stanislaus Kostka, and every year contributes to the bazaar in the latter parish. In a word, one can boldly say that the members of the Association will never refuse a contribution for the benefit of the parish or of a philanthropic purpose, and always actively participate in all parish affairs. The association arranges for its members every quarter a so-called Variety Evening, adorned not only with a supper but also with a program. The Association has been developing successfully from the day of its foundation up to the present and now numbers 388 active members. The financial statement shows $2,256.51 . . . .

UNITING THE IMMIGRANTS: "THE RESULTING ORGANIZATION WHILE SERVING THE PURPOSES OF THE POLISH CAUSE WILL BE NOT ONLY USEFUL BUT INDISPENSABLE FOR THE PRIVATE INTERESTS OF EVERY ONE OF ITS MEMBERS"

1879

> Agaton Giller's public letter to the Polish immigration in America outlined the successful formula for organizing the peasant-workers in the United States in their own interest and on behalf of the future of an independent Poland. His statement stimulated the formation of the Polish National Alliance in the next year. Giller was living in exile in Switzerland.

Since emigration exists and constitutes a great power -- a fact which cannot be denied -- it should be the task of a well understood patriotism to make it as useful as possible for the national cause. This can be done only through organization, which will unify the scattered members and control them in such a way that they will not be wasted but will be preserved for the fatherland . . . .

Every Polish peasant, from whatever Polish province he comes, even from one of those which like Upper Silesia or East Prussia have been for a long time separated from the national body, when transferred to a strange soil among foreigners develops a Polish sentiment and a consciousness of his national character. This phenomenon is incomprehensible for those who saw the peasant at home without a consciousness of national duties. And yet it is quite natural. National consciousness originates in him spontaneously in a foreign country in consequence of the feeling of the striking difference between his speech, his customs, his conceptions from those of the people who surround him. . . .

If after the formation of a conception and sentiment of nationality in him there is some one capable of explaining to him the meaning of this national character and of making him understand the duties resulting from this character then this plain man, formerly ignorant and passive for the national cause, will become an individual consciously and actively serving the idea which rests upon nationality . . . . There is, therefore, no doubt that if a national intellectual class is formed in America the numerous masses can and must be changed into an active human group useful for the national cause, and in order to give them the possibility of becoming useful and at the same time surround them with conditions which will prevent them from losing their nationality it is indispensable to unite the isolated individuals into more or less numerous associations and communities and bind these together in such a way that the resulting organization while serving the purposes of the Polish cause will be not only useful but indispensable for the private interests of every one of its members . . . .

When the mass of Poles in America is morally and nationally raised by the fact of being unified and is economically prosperous -- which should be also one of the tasks of the organization -- it will render great services to Poland, even by the mere fact of representing the Polish name well in America. These services can gradually become very considerable when the Poles begin to exercise an influence upon the public life of the United States, when they spread among Americans adequate conceptions about the Polish cause and information about the history, literature and art of our nation, when finally they become intermediaries between Poland and the powerful republic so as to foster sympathy with our efforts for liberation and develop it into an enthusiasm which will express itself in action.

Then only can happen that which is most desirable, i.e., the emigrants who have acquired training in practical lines and wealth in America will begin to return to their fatherland to be useful citizens . . . . We do not need to put forward those benefits which a large organization of Poles in America could bring at the decisive moment when the future of our fatherland will be at stake, for this is easy to see.

THE FUTURE OF THE IMMIGRANT: "WITH HOW MUCH DIGNITY WILL THE POLES WEAR ON THEIR HEADS THE CROWN OF AMERICAN CITIZENSHIP"

1881

The questions raised in this editorial in the first issue of Harmony (Zgoda), the official organ of the Polish National Alliance, have been asked ever since by the immigration in the United States. The answers -- a fairly rapid assimilation to middle class American life; an umbrella organization free of clerical domination; a vigorous defense of the Polish national cause -- were looked upon with deep suspicion by the conservative Catholic leadership of the immigration.

What awaits the Poles in America? In putting this question we have in mind the hundreds of thousands of Polish people scattered over the whole territory of the New World without any connection between them. One fact is striking. From among so many Polish emigrants not only not a single powerful personality has risen, but the average level has not even reached that of the most downtrodden European people, the Irish. The problem is thus with how much dignity will the Poles wear on their heads the crown of American citizenship. Will they remain behind the Irish and be only voting cattle, will they eternally continue to break stones, dig in mines, chop wood, drive mules, etc., or will they stand on the same level as Germans, Frenchmen, Englishmen in the higher professions, in literature, commerce, politics and the arts?. . . The solution of these problems will depend on the influence which the many various associations of Poles in this country exercise upon the mass of emigrants, for until the emigrants learn the English language these will be the only school in which the Poles coming to this country can educate themselves. We can be sure of one thing, that if our emigrants continue to submit, as they have done until now, to the influence of obscurantism [clericalism] , to the influence of those who for centuries have kept the people in blindness, they will never rise above the level of the Irish and the Polish name will never shine with any light in this country.

It is therefore necessary, first, that all existing Polish associations form one great national entity. Secondly, the Polish National Alliance should use the power of its organization to maintain an organ, a progressive periodical, which will enlighten and instruct the emigrant. It is necessary, further, that every commune organize a Polish library where the more educated will give lectures to their fellow-countrymen. At all celebrations of national anniversaries past and present Polish affairs should be discussed. With such means our emigrants will not only elevate their own spirits and rise above the level of the uneducated masses, but also will be better able to fulfil their mission with regard to Poland.

THE IDENTITY OF THE IMMIGRANT: "FAITH AS

THE BASIS OF POLONISM"

1913

This excerpt from Karol Wachtel's history of the Polish
Roman Catholic Union reviews the role of Roman
Catholicism in the evolution of Polish and Polish American
culture. It stands in contrast to the more secular view
of the founders of the Polish National Alliance.

The Polish Roman Catholic Union in America . . . . bears with justi-
fied pride the glorious slogans of Faith and Polonism, which have been for
centuries harmonized in our nation . . . .
Let us look at the fruits of our labor in this country, gathered in the
name of religion and nationality. We can, indeed, be proud of them, and
we are better in this respect than other peoples here, for probably none of
them has in so short a time gained so much for its cause or raised this
cause to such a flourishing condition as we have. Hundreds of Polish
parishes, hundreds of Polish schools and churches, hundreds of Polish
priests, a series of religious and national organizations and associations,
among them and at their head our splendid Roman Catholic Union grown under the aegis of Faith--all these work to maintain our standard and this
work does not consist in empty words, it is a work from dawn till night,
in church, in school, in association, in society in general, truly godly and
truly patriotic work. Who began it among us? Who is leading and spreading it? The Church. The Church through her servants, the priest
patriots, gives us the impulse and the opportunity for action. She teaches
us here that we are Poles, indicates how to behave to be worthy of this
name, gathers us around the hearth of nationality and faith and faithfully
defends her children from evil thought and subversive advice. The
Church does this; without it we should be nothing, as we were nothing
thirty years ago. Without it we should be lost for our fatherland, for the
national cause, for ourselves and our children . . . . To our forgotten and
unknown settlements in America came the priest from the fatherland.
He came like a missionary. He taught how to pray to God, how to read
Polish. He told them what Poland was, what the Polish people, their
national cause, for ourselves and our children . . . . To our forgotten and
unknown settlements in America came the priest from the fatherland.
He came like a missionary. He taught how to pray to God, how to read
Polish. He told them what Poland was, what the Polish people, their
national tasks and duties were. The priests raised churches, built schools
and hospitals, founded associations, inculcated the idea of concord and
unity, organized fraternal help. The priests created from chaotic and
dark masses a society which stands today, serious and strong, on the
foundation of its national existence, and goes forward with the same lead-

ing thought which lives in the heart of every Pole. That we are Poles, that we shall remain Poles to our death, that our children here will be Poles-this is the work of our religion. This is the merit of the Roman Catholic Church.

THE POLISH ROMAN CATHOLIC UNION: "THIS 'INSURANCE

ASSOCIATION' OFTEN BECOMES HERE THE GUARDIAN ANGEL

OF THE LONELY EMIGRANT''

1913

Karol Wachtel, in this passage from his history of the
PRCU, describes the contributions of the Union to the
ethnic life and social welfare of the immigrant.

Our opponents say about us that we are merely a mutual insurance society. If it is so, then all our alliances and unions here are mutual insurance societies. Moreover, all the non-Polish institutions of this type are
the same, for in view of the nature of American society and of its specific
inability to do anything without material interests they all have accepted
material propaganda and organization as a kind of foundation for their activities. Besides, even this material side has with us deeper and more
generous motives, motives of a purely humanitarian kind. Every insurance of ours is literally a benefit. . . . Taking into account the unusually low
assessments in the Union in proportion to the amount of insurance and considering, further, that besides this insurance the member receives for
the same money a whole series of other services which only the power of
association of a large number of people can give . . . . it will be seen that
this "insurance association" often becomes here the guardian angel of the
lonely emigrant and nearly takes the place of the mother-country which
he left . . . .

Let us look from still another side at this insurance. . . . We receive
here raw, simple, often very dark people . . . . You will not attract such
poor fellows who come here for bread by lofty ideas and high aspirations.
One of these has to be shown something practical, accessible to his understanding . . . . Only after being somewhat enlightened, raised and trained
by association with his fellow-countrymen he begins to feel a real Pole,
begins to talk about the need of education and is ready to give, if others
do, some money for this education or for Poland, the old country beyond the
ocean. This is how things are done here. This is how our society has developed . . . .

In the oldest constitution of the Union we read that the aim of the
organization is fraternal help of fellow-countrymen, the spreading and development of the spirit of brotherhood and of mutual confidence, the maintenance of Polonism, the fostering of civilization and Christian morality.
How did the Union fulfil these aims?. . . .

One of the most beloved causes, the object of the sincerest devotion
of the Union is education in parochial and higher schools . . . . The Union
has always been deeply interested in young people. Every year many
young members and societies of youth join the organization. The age

has been lowered to 14 years.   Former diets used to establish special commissions for propaganda among the youth -- all this because of the justifiable fear that the second generation unless attracted to Polonism in early youth will be lost for the national cause . . . .

Another branch of the work of our organization in the American Polonia was and is the maintenance of the patriotic spirit in people with the help of national celebrations and of the cult of our historical holidays and solemnities . . . .

Energetically and steadily the Union has counteracted all attempts of Americanization from whatever source they came. As an example we shall mention the characteristic affairs of 1901 when Bishop Eis of Marquette, Michigan, issued an order to teach religion in English in the parish schools, and a few other American bishops imitated his order.   These orders, however, provoked a series of protests from the clergy and the people. The Poles protested particularly strongly and among them the Union was one of the first to raise its voice. In a special memorial sent to the Apostolic delegate in Washington the reasons for the protest were set forth and the standpoint of the Poles was explained.   The latter respect the authority of the Church but they have fled across the ocean for the sake of their national liberties which they could not obtain in their own country. Will they be deprived of their native language here in a free country? . . . .

Among other affairs of the American Polonia in which the Union took a very prominent part was the effort to obtain equal rights for the Polish-American clergy in the hierarchy of the Church. The Poles have for a long time constituted a numerical and economic power among the Catholics of America, but even now they do not have proportionate representation among the higher Catholic clergy . . . . This affair was taken up by the Polish Catholic congresses, of which we had three, whose executive departments publicly and privately worked actively at Rome in order to break the prejudices and the opposition of Irish and German bishops.   The Union fostered whole-heartedly the Polish action, helped, for instance, to pay the cost of the delegation sent here to investigate the conditions . . . .

Everybody knows . . . that in the ruling spheres of the United States there is a strong tendency to limit immigration . . . . We defend ourselves as we can against these limitations of freedom of entrance into the country of Washington, which was guaranteed in the Constitution of the United States, and the Union has been energetically and efficiently participating in this defense.   [It sent memorials and delegations to Washington.]

THE CONSTITUTION OF THE POLISH NATIONAL ALLIANCE:

"A MORE PERFECT UNIFICATION OF THE POLISH EMIGRANTS"

1913

The Constitution of the National Alliance, adopted in 1913,
summarized a generation of experience in trying to meet
the social needs of the Polish immigrant and to integrate
him into the movement for Polish independence in Europe.

Introduction. When in spite of heroic sacrifices and bloody struggles
the Polish nation lost its independence, was condemned by the will of Providence to a triple slavery and forcibly deprived by its invaders of the
right to live and develop, that part of it which was most deeply wronged
preferred voluntary exile to the heavy slavery at home, wandered --
following the example of Kosciuszko and Pulaski -- to the free land of
Washington, and having settled here found hospitality and political and civil
rights. This brave handful of pilgrims without losing sight of their duties
with regard to their adopted country and nation founded the Polish
National Alliance. . . . .with the following aims: A more perfect unification
of the Polish emigrants, assistance in their economic, moral, intellectual
and social development, preservation of the native language, the national
culture and mores from decay, and more efficient action by all permissible
means in behalf of the independence of the Polish lands in Europe. Today,
therefore, desiring to stabilize further the foundations of this
Alliance we, the people of the Alliance and the delegates of the 20th diet,
gathered in Detroit, Michigan, September 18, A.D. 1913, as faithful guardians of the ideals which those founders transmitted to us a sacred heritage,
after an experience of thirty-three years confirm and promulgate these
fundamental statutes as the highest law equally binding all members belonging to the Polish National Alliance.

CHAPTER I

1. The highest legislative power of the Polish National Alliance
resides in the general diet . . . .
9. The diet cannot vote any law limiting the freedom of worship or
political convictions of the members of the Polish National Alliance . . . .

CHAPTER II

9. It is treason to the Polish National Alliance for a member to
incite or try to persuade other members, groups or departments to break
away from the National Alliance or violate its laws and rules; it is treason
to slander the Alliance or to harm it by representing in speech or writing
the aims, tendencies or interests of the Alliance in a false light . . . . The

penalty for treason to the National Alliance is expulsion from the organization and loss of all the rights, privileges and benefits of membership . . . .

10. No member, officer, group, committee, commission, department or part of the Alliance has the right to appeal to the courts of this country in affairs concerning the Alliance or any part of it until all the stages of jurisdiction and appeal within the Alliance, the diet included, have been exhausted.

CHAPTER VIII

1. The official language of the Polish National Alliance is the Polish language. . . .

CHAPTER XXIV

1. The Polish National Alliance will publish an official [weekly] organ named Zgoda, in which besides informatory and literary parts there will be special sections for particular departments and for the official announcements of the Alliance. In addition to the official organ a half-official [daily] organ named Dziennik Zwiazkowy will be published, which will give all information about the life of the Polish people at home and in foreign countries, watch over the interests of the Alliance and defend the weal of the Polish people.

5. The publications shall be edited in the Polish spirit in accordance with the postulates mentioned in the introduction to this constitution.

CHAPTER LVII

2. The Alliance has the following permanent commissions: The Commission of Enlightenment, the Commission of the Library and Museum, the Commission of Assistance, the Commissions of Emigration, the School Commission, the Commission of Industry and Labor and the Commission of Colonization.

3. . . . The duties of the Commission of Enlightenment are a) to grant loans without interest to sons or daughters of members studying in higher educational institutions; b) to hold literary contests; c) to furnish the libraries of the groups with selected works; d) to organize educational circles in localities where there are groups of the Alliance; e) in a word, to help by all possible means in every work aiming to spread education in Polish society in America . . . .

5. The duties of the Commission of Assistance are a) to give assistance to sick members who prove their need of assistance . . . b) to grant assistance to members who present certificates of complete destitution . . . c) to try to increase the assistance fund by all permissible means . . . .

6. The Commissions of Emigration . . . in ports. Their duties are a) to give assistance to the emigrants; b) to take care of the homes for emigrants. . . .

7. The School Commission is composed of as many persons as the charter of the College of the Polish National Alliance requires . . . . The Commission is to take care that the college be essentially national and the system of instruction is based on the education of the youth in a spirit of nationalism and citizenship.

THE IMMIGRANT LETTER: "I SEE YOU NOT,

AND I HEAR YOU NOT"

1909-1910

The immigrant himself was not always -- perhaps not usually -- concerned with the ideologies and struggles of his leaders. These letters illustrate some of his ordinary preoccupations. The first was written by a young scrub-girl at the Palmer House in Chicago to a friend at home; it suggests some of the loneliness of separation from the familiar things of one's youth. The second and third deal with the problems of the Polish family; they were written by the brother and the mother of an immigrant.

I

I am beginning this letter with the words: "Praised be Jesus Christ," and I hope that you will answer: "For centuries of centuries. Amen."

Dearest Olejniczka:

I greet you from my heart, and wish you health and happiness. God grant that this little letter reaches you well, and as happy as the birdies in May. This I wish you from my heart, dear Olejniczka.

> The rain is falling; it falls beneath my slipping feet.
> I do not mind; the post office is near.
> When I write my little letter
> I will flit with it there,
> And then, dearest Olejniczka
> My heart will be light, from giving you a pleasure.
> In no grove do the birds sing so sweetly
> As my heart, dearest Olejniczka, for you.
> Go, little letter, across the broad sea, for I cannot come to you.

When I arose in the morning, I looked up to the heavens and thought to myself that to you, dearest Olejniczka, a little letter I must send.

Dearest Olejniczka, I left papa, I left sister and brother and you to start out in the wide world, and to-day I am yearning and fading away like the world without the sun.

If I shall ever see you again, then, like a little child, of great joy I shall cry. To your feet I shall bow low, and your hands I shall kiss. Then you shall know how I love you, dearest Olejniczka.

I went up on a high hill and looked in that far direction, but I see you not, and I hear you not.

Dearest Olejniczka, only a few words will I write. As many sand-grains as there are in the field, as many drops of water in the sea, so many sweet years of life I, Walercia, wish you for the Easter holidays. I wish you all good, a hundred years of life, health and happiness. And loveliness I wish you. I greet you through the white lilies, I think of you every night, dearest Olejniczka.

Are you not in Bielice any more, or what? Answer, as I sent you a letter and there is no answer. Is there no one to write for you?

And now I write you how I am getting along. I am getting along well, very well. I have worked in a factory and I am now working in a hotel. I receive 18 (in our money 32) dollars a month, and that is very good.

If you would like it we could bring Wladzio over some day. We eat here every day what we get only for Easter in our country. We are bringing over Helena and brother now. I had $120 and I sent back $90.

I have no more to write, only we greet you from our heart, dearest Olejniczka. And the Olejniks and their children; and Wladislaw we greet; and the Szases with their children; and the Zwolyneks with their children; and the Grotas with their children, and the Gyrlas with their children; and all our acquaintances we greet.

My address: . . . .

Good-by. For the present, sweet good-by.

II

My dear Stas:

  You ask me for my opinion about marriage, and you ask about
[Miss] Swatowna. My brother, my Stas, I don't know what lot awaits
me. About this Swatowna, as you know, I tried so hard to gain her favor,
I took so many hard steps, and all this brought me nothing. I should have
come out all right there for, as this Miss Swatowna told me, she "gave
a basket" to Rudkowski because she loved me. But finally, when I expected to end the business, then my family began to find fault with it,
particularly mother. Well, I gave up the game, I stopped calling on her.
How they must talk about me there now! Swatowna is still a girl.
  I don't know now what will be the end of the hopes with which I still
deceive myself about the Kowalczyks in Czyzew. If God helped me, it
would be the best there. All this is in the hands of God. But it is a
hard nut to bite, for there is a crowd of various men around, and the
Kowalczyks themselves look upon this business from several sides. I
hear that they prefer me, but there was a time when things were so bad that
I said to myself that I wouldn't go there again. I was there a few times
and I never found her; evidently she hid herself. And she hid herself not
because she hated me, but because different marriage-brokers laughed
at her for receiving attention from me. Worse still, I noticed that the Kowalczyks began to treat me indifferently, particularly Mrs. Kowalczyk. This
observation pained me much, but what could I do?
  If I am to be successful with the Kowalczyks this money which you
speak of sending from America would be a great help. It would be necessary to show at least 2,000 roubles there, so if you sent your money I
would be that much bolder, because no stranger would know that it is
borrowed money. I say at least 2,000. It would be well to show have
5,000 cash of their own. I don't know, dear Stas, whether my efforts will
bring me happiness or irretrievable loss. O, my great God! I implore
you to help me . . . .

Wiktor Markiewicz

III

Dear Son:

Walenty in Dobrzykow, built a small mill upon his water in competition with us, but he grinds only three-quarters of once-ground flour a-day. Well, we don't know how it will be further. As to Elzbietka, she has a boy, a butcher from Lubien; I don't know whether she will marry him or not, but she says that this winter she will surely decide; if not this one, then another. I have trouble enough now for my sins. Always new guests, always some new fashion, always these new things, so that my income does not suffice. And you know that your father always says: "When anything is not there we can do without it." But sometimes it must be had, even if it must be cut out from under the palm of the hand! So, dear son, I beg you very much, if you can, send me a little money, but for my own needs. Elzbietka is grown up, Polcia is bigger still, Zonia begins to overtake them, and they all need to be dressed, while it is useless to speak to your father about it. If you can, send it as soon as possible, because if I sell some cow, or hog, or grain, it must be put aside. Your father says that it cannot be spent. We gave Pecia 100 roubles [when married] and 200, but we must still give 200 more. Bicia also [must have money] , so we must put money aside. Well, we have nice hogs, nice cattle and a nice horse, but I must work conscientiously for all this. Your father just excuses himself with his old age, and I may work with the children so that my bones crack. He says: "Then don't keep so much farmstock, don't work! Do I order you to do all this?" But when he wants anything, he has to have it. As to the crops, everything is not bad . . . . only we must work so much.

Everywhere only work and work, so that my bones lap over one another. But what can be done? Unfortunately my teeth decline absolutely to work any longer and I must have some new ones put in, but I have not money enough for it, for I have other things to spend it on. So if it is not a great detriment to you I beg you for a few roubles for my teeth. But if not, it cannot be helped. Well, grandmother wants to move to us now, but your father is honey and sugar and your grandmother is gall and pepper. Whoever has tried it knows the taste. Oh, all my life I have enjoyed this honey and this sugar! I have it often under every nail. But what can be done? It is the will of God . . . .

Your loving mother,

Anna Markiewicz

THE AMERICANIZATION OF AN IMMIGRANT: "I HOPE YOU WILL UNDERSTAND WHATE I MEAN"

1914

> This letter to an investigating commission in Massachusetts describes the dilemma of the immigrant worker who hoped to learn English and become Americanized in order to do better economically, the motive which probably first brought him to the United States.

I'm in this country four months (from 14 Mai 1913 -- Noniton Antverpen). I am polish man. I want be american citizen -- and took here first paper in 12 June N 625. But my friends are polish people -- I must live with them -- I work in the shoes-shop with polish people -- I stay all the time with them -- at home -- in the shop -- anywhere.

I want to live with american people, but I do not know anybody of american. I go 4 times to teacher and must pay $2 weekly. I wanted take board in english house, but I could not, for I earn only $5 or 6 in a week, and when I pay teacher $2, I have only $4-$3 -- and now english board house is too dear for me. Better job to get is very hard for me, because I do not speak well english and I cannot understand what they say to me. The teacher teach me -- but when I come home -- I must speak polish and in the shop also. In this way I can live in your country many years -- like my friends -- and never speak -- write well english -- and never be good american citizen. I know here many persons, they live here 10 or more years, and they are not citizens, they don't speak well english, they don't know geography and history of this country, they don't know constitution of America -- nothing. I don't like be like them I wanted they help me in english -- they could not -- because they knew nothing. I want go from them away. But where? Not in the country, because I want go in the city, free evening schools and lern. I'm looking for help. If somebody could give me another job between american people, help me live with them and lern english -- and could tell me the best way how I can fast lern -- it would be very, very good for me. Perhaps you have somebody, here he could help me?

If you can help me, I please you.

I wrote this letter myself and I know no good -- but I hope you will understand whate I mean.

Excuse me,

F. N.

THE VIEW FROM OUTSIDE: "AS A PEOPLE,

THEY HAVE BEEN MUCH ABUSED"

1916

This report by a social worker on a Polish neighborhood in
Philadelphia describes the problems of an immigrant
community. It bears comparison with Barbara Mikulski's
evaluation of these communities two generations later.

The foreign residents of our ward are principally Polish-Galatians,
Lithuanians, and those who come from Russian Poland. These people are
the most difficult of all the nationalities to deal with on account of their
handicap of language. Having been denied their own language by both
Germany and Russia, naturally there is no Polish language. The dialects
are so confused and mixed that even a knowledge of German and a knowledge of the Russian language does not enable you to make much headway
in conversing with them. After they come to this country and live together, 3,000 to 4,000 in a group, as in our district, they naturally form
a dialect of their own.

Our work was first to get them to attend the evening schools. This
was only done by opening the public school (the Wood) in the heart of the
district, so they would not have to go a long distance from the mills and
factories where they are employed and around which they live. Within
a week we had 160 in attendance at the school. These were two-thirds
adults: men and women past forty years of age, earning fair wages in
the mills, yet could not read or write a word of English. They could
speak fairly well, but had no reading or writing knowledge.

Our next work was visiting in the homes -- getting acquainted with the
mothers. The women are very much handicapped. They do not learn how
to prepare or cook American foods; how to buy the kind of clothing we
wear, which is best suited to their needs in this new land. Few have
books or papers to read from their own country. Thus these people, who
are expected to be the mothers of a new Poland in America, are shut off
from all the things that make life most worth living.

Our visitor, through the children as interpreters, first makes
friends with the mothers, then gradually teaches them what foods we consider most wholesome. We have a cooking class for them a part of the
year; also a girls' sewing class. We have had 15 Polish girls who work
in the mills and factories in this class for the past two years.

As our work is civic, the visitor connected with a public school is
always considered with the deference paid a teacher. It is hard to get
their interest, but once you make a Polish woman and family believe
you are their friend, they are most gratefully responsive. When the
visitor goes in the evening to make a friendly call, presumably upon the
children, the father talks with her, for in his workshop he has picked up
English. The pathetic part is that the woman always has to talk through the

child or the man and one cannot get at the root of her problem.

Last winter we hired a Polish woman to teach the girls sewing: this worked very well. We also have a class of school girls (Polish) who have cooking and housekeeping lessons taught under the auspices of the Civic Club. We call it a housekeeping center. In this class the girls learn quickly and take this training home to their mothers.

Summing up the work briefly, our accomplishments are: Securing a night school, where the adults and older boys and girls can learn English.

Teaching the girls cooking, housekeeping, sewing.

Instructing the mothers in the care of the children and babies.

Providing a nurse in the summer, who visits regularly and watches the babies during the heated weather.

Visiting -- Having a social visitor calling each week: going into the homes; teaching the mothers food values; how to get the most good from the money spent -- for where these women cannot come to us, we must go to them.

As a people, they have been much abused. In our locality where they live they are subjected to many abuses; the handicap of language makes them timid and shrinking; the German people with whom they mingle consider them only "the scum of the earth"; the low toughs of the neighborhood frequently waylay and rob them of their earnings as they go home at night. These men more frequently work at night. They are an industrious people. We find them honest -- they seldom owe rent, no matter how slack the work, and they rarely ask charity. But not understanding us, they fear our laws and more frequently get into trouble on account of their ignorance. It is no wonder they are blamed for so many crimes. A judge told me recently that his records were full of the names of Polish people; and that he considered them the most criminal of all Classes who come to our shores. This is partial libel: they are arrested, blamed, thrown into court; are usually compelled to have some unscrupulous lawyer who takes a tip from the other fellow and works against his Polish client. Thus the records may be full, but not always because the victim has committed the crime; rather because he is blamed for what he did not do.

These people are strong of body and have the sterling qualities of character needed to make them the right kind of American citizens. Work with them is slow, but with this group in the Fifteenth Ward our civic work is telling -- many of them are doing better and living better than they were two years ago.

Our plea now is for a wide-open school, such as they have in the congested sections of New York, where we can teach them many more things and where they can come every and any evening to learn the ways of our country. This year we have no night school for them. Our visitor is again canvassing the neighborhood in an effort to bring before the Board of Education sufficient signatures to warrant the school being opened. We consider the public school the best meeting-place for them, as they inherit the feeling that the "Schula" is all right.

THE IMMIGRANT AND POLAND: "THE AMERICAN POLONIA ...

UNTIL NOW HAS NOT BEEN VERY PRODUCTIVE

FOR THE POLISH CAUSE"

1913

Here, Karol Wachtel, in his history of the Polish Roman
Catholic Union, evaluates -- correctly -- the overall
impact of the American immigration before 1913 upon the
movement for Polish independence.

In order to complete the picture we must add a few details about the
role of the Union in general Polish affairs and its relation to the fatherland. Though we should sincerely like to write as much and as well as
possible about our activities in this field, which should be considered the
most important and essential since they concern the Polish cause itself,
although we should be glad to relate at length the merits of our institution,
impartiality compels us to confess that we must limit ourselves to a series
of passing manifestations, not very important in reality because not
systematically aiming at a stable policy for the future.

In saying this we hasten to mention that we have in mind not only the
Union. We speak in this case about the whole "fourth province," the
American Polonia, which until now has not been very productive for the
Polish cause though there are already beginnings, promising a better
state of affairs in the near future. Up to the present everything which the
American Polonia has done for Poland has certainly been very well meant
very sympathetic but without permanent value. They were only sporadic
and isolated manifestations, a few relief offerings, some expressions of
indignation and sympathy for the lot of our fellow-countrymen in the
fatherland, a few attempts to help arranged without sufficient preparation-
that is all which can in general be said about the service of American
Poles to their mother-country.

THE WORLD WAR AND POLAND: "PROTEST OF THE POLISH WOMEN'S ALLIANCE AGAINST PEACE AT ANY PRICE"

1915

At a women's peace conference at The Hauge in 1915, the delegates of the Polish Women's Alliance of America worked to make the restoration of Poland an important objective of the international peace movement. The continued division of Poland, they argued, was an injustice and a threat to the stability of Europe.

Owing to a systematic spreading of the propaganda of "Peace at any Price,'' we call to all who do not know the pangs of exile -- to all who never suffered the torments of tyranny -- to all who have not felt the pains of oppression -- to all who believe in humanity, justice and liberty, that:
Peace -- without reparation of wrongs for centuries perpetrated on subdued nations -- Peace, without justice to their immortal laws of life and liberty -- Peace, regardless of oceans of blood and tortures without number -- deaths innumerable for the upholding of law and justice -- such peace would be a new crime of nations and an everlasting shame on our civilization. It would be a sacrilege for the holy sacrifices incurred by this war.
Among the martyr-nations in the first ranks stands Poland feloniously torn asunder in the past century. Poland, the buffer State of Western civilization -- the Knights of Nations, the oldest warrior for the cause of freedom and justice -- today again by violence and force thrown into horrible combat with each of the enemy-armies, changed into a desert by passing soldiery without number, carrying on their titanic struggle in our own lands . . . .
Poland today is like Lazarus, thrown on the bed of blood, fire and embers -- murdering her own children by order of her enemies -- sinking the steel in the breasts of her own sons, fathers and brothers . . . .
In view of this terrible tax of blood, property and life devoured by war from our own unhappy nation, which is a crime of humanity and the world -- we, the daughters of this downtrodden and blood bespattered unhappy country, do raise our mighty voice of mothers, daughters, sisters and wives suffering beyond measure, calling to all nations:
"Create a peace of the world, but a new kind of peace lasting and holy -- not as heretofore founded on injury, misery and violence, on the breaking of laws and enslaving the weaker nations, such a peace must be compensated by most bloody wars, oceans of fire, smoke and annihilation -- create a new peace, a peace that will declare to all the world that all harm and grievances are forgotten, that slavery has fallen, that violence and injury are no more, a peace that will hail a new world existence."
It was that kind of peace our Polish Delegates demanded at Peace Congress at the Hague, and by an appropriate resolution the women of the world demanded such a peace.

For such a new kind of peace, founded on humanity and justice, will honor law and order and promote happiness of all humankind -- will end strife and slavery and violence among cultured nations -- will for all time stop the cruel torture of the weaker by the stronger.

We, the daughters of a nation whose freedom was seized by force and most brutal violence, being in reality a daylight robbery, with one united voice protest with all our soul against all false-peace action and activity whose ultimate is peace at any price."

THE END OF THE WAR: "THE POLISH NATIONAL ALLIANCE HAS

BEEN VICTORIOUS ON THE WHOLE FRONT"

1918

At the end of World War I, President Zychlinski of the
Polish National Alliance was able to look back with pride
on the steadfast and successful Polish policy of his organization. Here, in his report to the convention of the
Alliance, he reviews the startling reversal in the fortunes
of Poland in the last two years.

. . . . I begin my report with the political standpoint of the National
Alliance during the last three years, for on this standpoint depended not
only the financial and numerical development of the organization but its
very future existence. I shall never forget the end of the year 1916 and
the beginning of 1917 when my office was flooded with letters from members of the Alliance demanding a revision of our standpoint and subordin-
ation to our country   [Poland] , for only our country could decide the
political standpoint of Poles at home and abroad . . . . Great was the
Prussian bait in the form of the Austrian-German manifesto published on
November 5, 1916   proclaiming the independence of Poland   . . . . At
the same time the Central Powers were at the summit of their military
power . . . . It seemed that all the hopes based on the Allies were falling
to the ground . . . but we stood firm . . . . And today with joy and pride I
can say that the Polish National Alliance has been victorious on the whole
front, that it has not betrayed or thrown away the aims of its founders but
has remained true to them to the end, and has lived to see the already victorious Allies accept as the main point of peace the demand for a free,
unified and independent Poland with an access to the sea. I am persuaded
that all the members of the Alliance share my pride and joy . . . . for
although the Polish National Alliance has become only the leading part of
the enormous Polish machine organized by the emigrants in order to give
our fatherland financial and military help, nevertheless our organization
has had an almost decisive voice in the most important affairs bearing
on the position and the future of the Polish nation . . . .

The benefits which the Polish National Alliance in particular and the
Polish people in general have received from this victory are so numerous
that I cannot enumerate them all. I shall only mention the most important
ones . . . . First of all, in the mass of the people of the Alliance self-
confidence and trust in the leading elements of the organization have been
firmly established. While in the politically uncertain period between the
20th and 21st diets the numerical growth of the Alliance was relatively
small in spite of the fact that the emigration from Poland, though dimin-
ished, still continued, during the period preceding this diet the increase in
membership was more than 20,000 notwithstanding the entire lack of
emigration, the enrollment of hundreds of thousands of Polish youths

under the American standards, the voluntary enlistment of thousands of them under Polish standards and the deplorable arguments of those intending to return to Poland who claim that it is not worth their while to become insured. An even greater difference is noticeable in the financial status of our organization, for during these three years the property of the Alliance was almost doubled, which means that all groups willingly paid their obligations, feeling sure that their leaders would not disappoint them . . . .

From the very first moment of the organization of the Polish army the central administration of the Alliance devoted much attention to it and hastened to help whenever this was possible . . . . For this Polish army is the realization of one of the fundamental aims of the Polish National Alliance which even before the war prepared the Polish youth for this military action by surrounding the Sokols with its protection . . . .

Our organization has also with its whole heart promoted the war of the United States against our hereditary foe, Germany. Not only did numerous volunteers from the ranks of the Alliance enlist under the Star Spangled Banner, not only did I visit personally these volunteers in Jefferson Barracks, instilling spirit into them and placing Polish ideals before their eyes, but when the government appealed to the people for financial help . . . the Polish National Alliance bought $150,000 worth of liberty bonds, $5,000 of war savings stamps and through its organs developed such a propaganda that the people of the Alliance led all Polish organizations in the purchase of these bonds. The government of the United States recognized this effort and sent to the central administration special thanks for the activity of the Alliance, full not only of loyalty but of real patriotism.

POLISH AMERICA AND THE FUTURE OF POLAND: "WE HERE MUST BE

OFFICIALLY FIRST OF ALL AMERICANS--OF POLISH ORIGIN AND WITH

SINCERE POLISH SYMPATHIES, BUT AMERICANS"

1919

One year after the end of the World War and the restoration of Poland, Karol Wachtel's article in the
Chicago Polish Daily News (Dziennik Chicogoski) signaled
clearly the new relationship between the immigration
and the old homeland.

On the eve of the second general diet of the Polish emigrants in
America, which will meet next week in Buffalo, N. Y., we wish to express
briefly and clearly our opinion about the most important question that
this diet is going to decide, the question whether our National Department
here should continue to exist or should be closed . . . . We do not see any
need of dragging in this organization, which is wholly artificial and not
based on the real relation of the forces active in Polish-American society.
In view of this we express here the opinion of our paper that . . . . the
National Department should honorably close its existence and disband.
In expressing this opinion we speak not only for ourselves, not only for
this one paper but for numerous masses of our society, for many circles
of our citizens . . . . The political situation is now entirely different from
that which was the background for calling the department to life and action.
None of the needs for which the Department was created exist now either
in the political or the economic, or in any other domain.

The political affairs will be taken entirely away from us and should
be taken away in order that now when our state exists and must carefully
guard its political dignity its course be not troubled by our dilettantism,
which has caused considerable harm even during the period when we were
doing our best work here. Politics will henceforth be conducted by our
fatherland and its givernment and its foreign representative, the Polish
embassy in Washington. We shall not mix into political matters and
shall have not the slightest right to do so. Up to the present America
could tolerate our Polonistic tendencies because they were based on the
political program of Wilson with reference to Poland. But now, when
the fundamental Polish ambitions have been realized, our role automati-
cally ends and returns to its proper field. It should be clearly recognized
that we here must be officially first of all Americans -- of Polish origin
and with sincere Polish sympathies, but Americans; and this excludes any
politics which are not purely American.

In economic and humanitarian matters the field will also rapidly
diminish. The relief activity is approaching its end. For the humanitarian work another kind of activity, much more important and more

valuable morally and materially, should be substituted -- we mean activity in such domains as commerce and industry. But for this the Department will not be needed. Up to the present it has done absolutely nothing in these domains and its Commission of Commerce has remained literally a "paper commission." This group of activities will be the object of the Polish consuls, who will deal directly with Polish firms, cooperative organizations, etc . . . .

There is little to be said about other affairs. There may be something still to do about influencing American opinion in favor of Poland, but in this line unhappily all the former activities of the National Department were completely insignificant, and the results reached by it are infinitesimal. We shall not discuss whether this was due to lack of forces, of abilities or of will. The fact is that this field has been fatally neglected and in many cases to the great detriment of our cause (the Jewish, Lithuanian and Ukrainian questions) . . . .

We maintain thus our opinion that at the diet the role of the National Department should be declared finished and this organization dissolved. We shall have to go without it in the future, and we shall be able to do it . . . We possess in our Polonia powerful and well stabilized organizations. These after resigning the wide fields of political and social activity mentioned above will be very well able to manage the particular local affairs. The work will be certainly at any rate in accordance with the general program of regeneration of our national life. Our patriotic bonds, our sincerely Polish spirit will remain in us, will not be abolished by the abolition of the Department, and peaceful, noble emulation in the social and national work will benefit both American Polonia and Poland.

WORLD WAR AND COLD WAR: "POLAND'S CASE IS A CRITERION OF INTERNATIONAL MORALITY"

1945

> No issue did more to create difficulties within the anti-German coalition during World War II than the future of Poland. By 1944, Polish American leaders, struggling to preserve the boundaries and government of pre-war Poland, had concluded that the Soviet Union was the chief obstacle to their aims. The Soviet-American alliance was bound to lose favor in their view. This protest by the Polish American press, made shortly after the Yalta Conference, reflects their disappointment with the outcome of the war and anticipates many of the issues and outlooks of the Cold War in the late 1940's.

At a conference of the United Polish-Language Press in America held in Chicago, February 18, 1945, representatives of all Polish-American newspapermen's organizations resolved to address themselves to their colleagues in an open letter, to make their opposition to the Yalta decision regarding Poland known to their fellow newspapermen.

We speak in the name of hundreds of thousands of American soldiers of Polish origin now serving in our armed forces, in the name of their families, their fallen comrades in arms, and their children, and in the name of hundreds of thousands of farmers and laborers engaged in our war industry. Our newspapers are read by members of 800 parishes and their priests.

The Polish-language press, serving a large part of our nation, has a rich record of more than a half-century of patriotic work in every civic field.

It has been our job to interpret America to millions of immigrants whom we have assisted in the complicated process of adjustment and Americanization. We are proud of the results knowing that we have given America a very large group of loyal citizens who became an integral part of our nation.

We are Americans whose distinction is our Polish origin, our knowledge of the history, culture, psychology, traditions, and language of the country of our parents. We descend from thousands of noble idealists who came to America to fight at the side of Washington, whose birthday we are celebrating today. Kosciuszko, Pulaski, Krzyzanowski, Karge--great soldiers and patriots have fought for the independence and freedom of this country: thousands of unknown Poles have joined them then in the supreme sacrifice on the altar of our republic. This heritage of idealism and loyalty is now the common spiritual wealth of every one of those of Polish origin, whose names appear daily in the press among those killed, wounded, or decorated for valor.

You may well ask why the Polish-language press so ardently defends Poland, suggesting perhaps in this question a veiled insinuation that our attitude is any way un-American or hyphenated American.

To this we have many answers. It is not only the Polish-language press that defends Poland's rights. A large part of the English-language press in this country takes the same attitude, the only attitude dictated by American tradition and spirit. Our affection for the country of our fathers does in no way interfere or conflict with our love and devotion towards the United States.

In defending Poland's cause we express the emotions and determination of millions of men and women whose close relatives are the victims abroad.

We know Russia from centuries of experience, very close contact, and from history. These are some of the reasons, yet the most important one is our deep conviction that the role now accepted by the United States regarding Europe is fraught with the danger of tragic consequences for America.

We have surrendered, we have appeased, we have engaged ourselves in a speculation of the future based on illusions and passing exigencies, we have sown the seeds of a third world war, we have abandoned principles and accepted formulas.

Not so very long ago our government stated its policy, namely, that the United States will recognize no territorial changes in Europe -- yet we approved and undersigned the fifth partition of Poland.

We have traditionally refused to recognize any grab of land made by force of arms -- yet here, while Russia's invasion of Poland in 1939 and her subsequent incorporation of half of Poland is undoubtedly an abuse of force and an act of force -- we departed from our noble tradition and recognized might as right.

Our State Department expressed the will of the United States that territorial disputes be settled by an international organization after the war -- yet at Yalta we departed from that decision and from the will of the nation, settling now -- as demanded by Russia -- the fate and future of an ally in his absence, without hearing his case, without consulting or respecting other nations.

Before Yalta our State Department declared that it recognized the Polish government in London, on the basis that to that government belongs the credit for the five long years of Poland's resistance to Hitler, and for the gallant contribution made by the Polish armies everywhere. If no other reasons were sufficiently convincing, this alone, the war record of the Polish state, nation, and armed forces is sufficient ground why the Polish government in London should be recognized. Yet at Yalta we recognized the puppet government of Lublin and helped dress it up with a few new rags to hide the ugly truth.

We are partners in the fateful job of creating a new order in Europe solely because of Russia's military power and unyielding cynicism. That was not our aim nor does that justify the presence and sacrifices of hundreds of thousands of our boys on European soil.

The moral principles of the Atlantic Charter have been discarded, the idea of collective security has been pigeonholed, any attemp of cooperation, consultation, or agreement of all the United Nations has been frustrated.

We have been forced into a position of humiliating subservience in matters vital to the future of the world. We see in this policy now openly endorsed a grave danger to the future of the world and to the noble aims to which we have dedicated ourselves.

Poland's fate is a clear and tragic proof of it.

We therefore declare ourselves in opposition to the provisions regarding Poland contained in the Yalta agreement.

We shall continue to fight within our rights and privileges under a democracy for justice to Poland.

We shall continue to recognize the Polish government in London as representing Poland as a state and the Polish nation as an ally.

We shall continue to appeal to our fellow Americans not to abandon Poland. You, our colleagues, are the first ones to whom we address ourselves in our anxiety that with the victory of our arms, democracy, justice, and American ideals should also win.

Poland's case is a criterion of international morality, of our aims and achievements in this war. We see in the decision reached at Yalta a grave warning to America that our aims are seriously jeopardized and our future role in Europe doomed to failure if we permit facts to be accomplished before the establishment of a world organization.

America has made decisions without giving guarantees. America has taken responsibilities which engage her morally in future protection of the victims of her decisions, should they be violated at any time by anybody. This clearly binds the United States not only legally but also historically by an act which prejudices a prior position in an international body.

We plead with you, dear colleagues, to consider these facts and to appreciate Poland's case in the light of these and many other serious considerations. You will, we are sure, find that the Polish-language press in America judges those facts in anxious forebodings regarding the inevitable consequences that may affect both the United States and the future of the rest of the world.

We want to register with you our judgment that the fifth partition of Poland is a travesty of justice and will go down in history as did the other partitions. We should be grateful to you for an opportunity to discuss this matter with you personally.

EDMUND MUSKIE: "THIS IS OUR HERITAGE"

1966

Senator Muskie, the most important American politician of Polish descent, delivered this review of the Polish heritage at Alliance College on May 7, 1966, the year of the Polish Millenium. It reflects the conventional wisdom of Polish Americans about their specific European heritage -- which alone would make it a significant summary -- and, besides, attempts to relate that heritage to the civil rights and minority rights movements of the 1960's.

We are here because, one thousand years ago, Poland entered upon the stage of world history -- and embraced Christianity.

Ever since, she has had an impressive and meaningful influence upon Western civilization.

An influence that has enriched the life of Western man.

An influence that has contributed to the development of Western political institutions and concepts.

An influence that has been exerted by Polish leaders who have been, at the same time, leaders in the Western World.

An influence that gives us reason, as Poles, on this millennium anniversary, to be proud of our heritage and what it has meant for mankind.

It is appropriate, therefore, that we should create occasions such as this to review that heritage, to take satisfaction from it, but more important, to draw meaning from it as we contemplate today's world and the unknown future.

There is much of glory in Poland's past -- glory which was the product of the love of liberty, fierce independence, intense patriotism, and courage so characteristic of the Polish people.

And because of her geographic position, Poland has had ample opportunity to put these qualities to the test.

On two important occasions in a thousand years, Poland was the first line of defense against invading hordes from the East. She held her line proudly, and the eastern dreams of conquering Europe were dashed.

Every Pole remembers that in 1241, Prince Henryk Pobozny at the cost of his life forced the Mongol invaders to retreat to Asia in the battle of Legnica.

Every Pole remembers that, in 1683, Poland put an end to Turkish expansion in Europe, when the great Jan Sobieski went to the aid of Vienna, and, in a decisive battle, routed the Turks.

And no Pole will ever forget that, even under the burdens Poland has carried in this century, she has fought gallantly in the cause of freedom.

In 1920, Polish armies, led by Marshal Jozef Pilsudski, arrested the march of the Bolsheviks on Germany, and the victory, known as the "miracle on the banks of the Vistula," was credited with saving Europe from communism.

In 1939, Poland was the first to feel the military heel of the Nazis at the start of World War II.

Outmatched at the start by Germany's motorized military machine, Poland was stung 17 days later by an attack on the East front by Russia.

Alone and isolated, unable to defend herself on her homeland, she refused to play a passive role in the war.

Without delay, the Polish Army, Navy and Air Force, 80,000 strong, regrouped in France, fought at the side of France, then with the British, and later on, in Norway, North Africa, Italy, Normandy, Belgium and the Netherlands. In the famous battle of Britain in 1940, Polish airmen were responsible for 15 percent of the German air losses. Altogether, more than 300,000 Poles served with the Allied forces during the war. Meanwhile, at home, Poland built one of the strongest underground networks in Nazi-occupied Europe.

This is a valiant record for a nation which was attacked and overrun by two nations almost before the rest of the world recognized that a global war had begun.

It is the record of a nation which, for a thousand years, has never rejected the burdens of freedom. And despite the bitter disappointments of the postwar years, the spirit of freedom has never died. The Poznan uprising of 1956 was a vivid expression of that spirit. It still burns today among Poles, both in and out of Poland, and always will.

The same qualities which brought glory on the field of battle, were the inspiration for achievement in the works of peace.

Poland's history sings of human and cultural progress.

Encouraged by centuries of reverence for individual freedom, the arts and sciences flourished.

Even a partial list is impressive:

Europe's first ministry of education resulting from the constitution of 1791;

Mikolaj Kopernik, one of Europe's outstanding scholars in the 16th century, and the father of modern astronomy;

Ludwik Zamenhoff, the inventor of the language of Esperanto;

Madame Marie Curie-Sklodowska, world-famous for the discovery of radium;

In the field of literature, Wladyslaw Reymont and Henryk Sienkiewicz, winners of Nobel Prizes, Reymont for his novel "The Peasants," and Sienkiewica for "Quo Vadis"; and the world renowned Jozef Conrad-Korzeniowski, author of "Lord Jim" and other novels.

In no field has the glory of Poland shone more brightly than in the field of music. Frederic Chopin is a gift to the ages. His brilliant compositions will delight the souls of men as long as music is heard. And in our times, the world has thrilled to the incomparable Paderewski, Rubenstein, Landowska, and Rodginski.

These glories are but the beginning of the Polish story.

Especially impressive have been Poland's contributions to the ideals and concepts of democracy.

In the 15th, 16th, and 17th centuries, Poland was the largest and most civilized and powerful state in Central and Eastern Europe.

And the significant fact is that this achievement was built on a series of fundamental concepts of liberty:

The "Neminem Captivabimus" in 1425 which guaranteed personal liberty of the citizens.

The "Statutes of Niesazawa" in 1454 which established a bicameral parliamentary system.

The "Nihil Novi" in 1505 which made the crown powerless to legislate without consent of the two chambers.

Beginning in 1573, election of the kings of Poland, and a new set of laws known as "Pacta Conventa" which gave citizens the right to withdraw allegiance to the king if he transgressed any law or broke any stipulation under which he was elected.

These and other concepts are striking examples of a nation's will to be free of tyranny.

It was the custom for nations seeking empires to subjugate weaker nations and to build autocratic central authority.

Not in Poland. Internally, she decentralized authority. Internationally, she sought to win the hearts of her member nations. She undertook to gain their loyalty, not by coercion, but by making them political and cultural partners.

The free union of Poland and Lithuania, concluded in 1413, is unique in the history of international relations. The treaty puts at the very basis of the union the Christian principle of love.

An attitude of tolerance and respect for local institutions, religion and language was taken by Poland toward her vassal states.

The immense dominions of the Polish crown were divided into 34 provinces, all of which enjoyed all the privileges and benefits of broadly conceived self-government.

Eventually, the degree of local independence contributed to the several partitions of Poland in the 18th century. However, she responded to the internal turmoil by writing the constitution of 1791, a remarkable document in its day. It balanced individual freedoms against the needs of the nation.

Class distinction was ended. Towns obtained administrative and judicial autonomy and parliamentary representation. Peasants were placed under the protection of law. Measures aimed at the abolition of serfdom were sanctioned.

What is there, then, in all this thousand years of history as a Christian nation which has particular pertinence to our day, to our times, and to our future?

Belief in God -- yes -- with a faith which relates God's will and God's justice and God's compassion to the destiny of Poles and Poland -- as in that great national symbol -- the black madonna.

And so Poles have believed in and fought for the dignity of man -- as they have believed in and fought for the independence of Poland -- and as they have believed in and fought for freedom from tyranny.

These beliefs have written our history, inspired our leaders and our people, shaped our institutions, produced our culture, our literature and our music. These beliefs are Poland -- the Poland which the world knows and honors and respects -- the Poland of history! -- the Poland which lives in the hearts and minds of all Poles!

This is the Poland which, in the Warsaw Conference of 1573, guaranteed free worship of any religion.

This is the Poland, whose non-Jewish Poles, hid 300,000 Jews from the searching German Nazis, notwithstanding the threat of the death penalty if caught.

This is the Poland whose Tadeusz Kosciuszko, the "father of American artillery," fought for American independence and then authorized the sale of the lands given him by a grateful America, the proceeds to be used to free and educate slaves.

This is the Poland whose Kasimir Pulaski, the "father of American cavalry," died in the same cause.

This is the Poland of which my father spoke to me, at his knee, for hours on end, out of the fullness of his heart.

Increasingly, as the years passed by and my comprehension grew, he drove home his lesson. What he had lost by leaving Poland had been more than offset by what he gained -- for himself and for me. Here, if a man had ability, he could apply it in a manner of his own choosing. Here, if a man had an opinion, he could express it without fear of reprisal. Here, if a man disagreed with governmental policy, he could say so, and, more than that, he could do something about it by casting his ballot at the polls. Here, a man was completely free to reap the fruits of his own integrity, intellectual and physical capacity, his own work. There were no heights toward which he could not strive. It mattered not what his national background, his religious or political beliefs, his economic status in life might be.

These beliefs were my father's life. He held them confidently through periods when he felt the lash of prejudice directed against those of foreign birth and of his creed. On the evening of my inaugural day as Governor of Maine, he turned to me and said, very simply, "Now I can die happy." A few months later the final chapter of his life was written. I am sure that, in the closing moments, he must have thought of the strange and wonderful destiny which had so astonishingly vindicated the beliefs which had uprooted his life.

In 1789, Benjamin Franklin described the America which was my father's life, and his Polish heritage when he wrote:

"God grant, that not only the love of liberty but a thorough knowledge of the rights of man, may pervade all the nations of the earth, so that a philosopher may set his foot anywhere on its surface, and say, 'this is my country.' " This is our heritage -- and our unfinished task -- here and around the globe.

Everyone in America is a member of a minority group. It may be economic, social, political, religious, racial, regional, or based upon national origin. It may not be such today as to set us apart in any unpleasant way. But it could tomorrow!

Our particular minority group may be joined today with others in a common cause or common prejudice or a common indifference with majority status. The accompanying power to affect the rights and privileges of minority groups not a part of the coalition is subject to abuse resulting from indifference, callousness, or deliberate intent.

Today, as a member of the current majority, the possibility, or even the actuality, of such abuse may be of no concern to us. But it could be, if our particular minority group becomes the object of tomorrow's prejudice or indifference!

To those who say -- and there are such -- that certain national and ethnic groups are better and more desirable as Americans than others, let us ask: "Who is to make the selection, and at what point in history, and is the selection subject to revision as the majority coalition changes?"

To those who say that there are superior and inferior citizens, depending wholly upon race, national origin, religion, or color, let us ask, "Who is to make the selection and how can you be sure what your status will be when the majority coalition takes shape?"

I am not suggesting that the case for civil liberties should be based upon fear of each other.

I am saying simply this. Our differences have made our country great. They have done so because, increasingly, creative ability, intellectual capacity, and high moral and spiritual principles, wherever found, have been allowed to seek their highest attainable level.

I am also saying this. Our differences can destroy us; and the instruments for such destruction are prejudice, fear, indifference, hatred and retaliation.

Is it better for us and our country that we seek reasons to like and trust each other? Or is it better that we seek reasons to fear each other?

In the 1860's, the Maine legislature concerned itself with the problem of inducing settlements in the unpeopled townships of the State. An agent was sent to Sweden, with instructions to make vigorous efforts to establish a Swedish colony in Maine. Within ten weeks he had brought to Maine twenty-two men, eleven women and eighteen children -- including a pastor, farmers, a civil engineer, a blacksmith, two carpenters, a basket maker, a baker, a tailor and a shoemaker. They carved a home out of the wilderness of northern Maine.

New immigrants followed. Within five years the population had increased to 600 who had built a prosperous community of 130 houses, barns, two steam sawmills, one water power sawmill and the incidental business establishments. At the end of five years, 133 men applied for citizenship.

A member of the Swedish Parliament wrote to the Governor of Maine as follows: "May the young colony of the 'New Sweden' grow and flourish not only in material strength, but even in developing their moral and intellectual faculties. And may the new population thus add to your state and to your great republic a good and healthy element of moral power from the old world, and becoming imbued with the spirit of your free institutions, reflect that spirit on their native land.

"What we have lost in the old fatherland will then not have been lost to humanity: On the contrary, the trees have only been transplanted on a fresher soil, where they will thrive better, and give richer and more abundant fruits. God bless the harvest. God bless your land."

And we are the new Poland--with a similar mission.

Civil liberty is the sunshine without which the crop will suffer. The enemy of civil liberty is prejudice. The cause of prejudice is fear-- fear of the unknown, fear that there is no real basis for mutual trust and confidence, fear that those discriminated against may abuse power and authority if given the chance.

If such fears are well-founded, there is no real basis for democratic institutions. All the evidence from our national history and experience indicates that they are not well-founded. The growth of our free institutions -- their effectiveness and strength -- has been in direct proportion to the expansion of civil liberties and their enjoyment by greater numbers of our people of more diverse and varied backgrounds, talents, and experiences. This has been our harvest. And it has been fruitful.

The cause of civil liberties, then, is not simply that of do-gooders, or of neighbors interfering without justification in the affairs of neighbors. It is the cause of all those who are concerned that our national climate be a healthy one.

Let those who support this cause, however, avoid self-righteousness. Let us not refuse to give the trust and confidence which we ask. Faith begets faith if buttressed by an accumulation of reassuring experiences.

We have made legislative progress in this field in recent years. Some believe we have moved too fast; others that we have not moved fast enough. Without resolving that difference of opinion, I think it fair to say that we have moved ahead, that the movement has achieved constructive results, and that it gives promise of more progress.

And we should take pride as Poles, that, as we contribute to that progress, we will be enhancing an ancient Polish heritage -- a heritage that was nobly expressed in 1413 in the treaty of union between Poland and Lithuania:

"May this deed be remembered forever. It is known to all that he will not attain salvation who is not sustained by the mystery of love which -- radiates goodness, reconciles those in discord, unites those who quarrel, dissipates hatred, puts an end to anger, furnishes to all the food of peace, brings together the scattered, lifts up the fallen, makes rough way smooth, turns wrong into right, aids virtues, injures no one, delights in all things: he, who take refuge in its arms will find safety, and thenceforth even though insulted, will have no fear.

"Through love, laws are established, kingdoms are ruled, cities are set in order, and the welfare of the state is brought to its highest."

This is the creed of a Christian nation.

We believe it because it is right.

We believe it because we are God's children.

We know that, only when all God's children are warmed by its beneficient glow, can we hope to achieve justice, and order, and peace on earth.

EUGENE KUSIELEWICZ: "REFLECTIONS ON THE CULTURAL

CONDITION OF THE POLISH AMERICAN COMMUNITY"

1969

These remarks were delivered at a Convention of Polish
American Scholars at Alliance College. They are a view
from within, both critical of the Polish American heritage
and conscious of its importance and value. Kusielewicz,
a native born American, succeeded Stephen Mizwa as
president of the Kosciuszko Foundation in 1970.

During the last few weeks, I came across the observations of two
Polish American scholars on the current cultural climate within the
Polish American Community. Working independently, in two different sections of the country, they arrived at almost identic conclusions. As they
are germane to the subject of our meeting I take the liberty of presenting
their observations.

The first set of observations are by Dr. Marie Gutowska, who has
taught at the University of Massachusetts for over twenty years. They
appear in the first chapter of her unpublished manuscript entitled Glimpses
into the Story of Polish Americans. She writes:

The second generation of Poles in America, the first to be born
in the United States, was for the most part educated in American
schools. They responded readily to social progress, and showed
a rising level of cultural growth. The Polish language was still
spoken at home, but they soon realized that the vocabulary was
small and the colloquialism and Americanisms, large. At school
nothing was ever said about the contributions made by their kind to
American Society. Therefore, the only parts of their heritage
they knew were the already mentioned folk-dances, folk-songs,
special foods and a few prayers at church. The able and alert
youngsters could not be satisfied by this and soon some made the
oversimplified generalization that there is nothing to be proud of
in their Polish ancestry. When these children grew up, many tried
to forget all about their family background. Many changed their
name. An inferiority complex was often found among them, as
well as the loss of a sense of togetherness with the Polish ethnic
group. The problem of their Polish descent became an annoyance
to them and psychological difficulties developed in many cases.
There was a general confusion among them about the value of their
so-called "Polish Heritage."

The second set of observations are by Dr. Kolm, of the faculty of
the Catholic University of America's School of Social Services. In an

article entitled "The Identity Crisis of Polish-Americans" that appeared
in the April-June 1969 issue of The Quarterly Review, the official publication of the American Council of Polish Cultural Clubs, he writes as
follows:

> There was timidity and self-consciousness among the students
> about their ethnic background. Their academic performance was
> generally above average, often superior, but in class they were the last
> to speak up. They identified themselves as Polish-Americans only
> after several weeks of classes and only in private. Once a relation-
> ship was established there were many questions, with a general tone
> of anxiety about their loss of Polish identity. They knew little
> about Poland, past or present. They usually had some cliches about
> poverty and backwardness in Poland from the grandparents. Most
> spoke only a few words of Polish but understood the spoken word
> well. Some were quite fluent but reticent with this skill.
>
> This could be ominous if we add some other facts, such as the
> largest number of changed names of any ethnic group, the rapid dis-
> appearance of the Polish language from parochial schools and church-
> es, the decrease of Polish newspapers.
>
> Disregarding gloomy predictions, the timidity of Polish Ameri-
> cans regarding their cultural background is the single most important
> factor in the problem of cultural identity. It confirms similar ob-
> servations by Dr. Kusielewicz and others about feelings of infer-
> iority and a generation gap in Polish American institutions.

Generally, Polish Americans, and particularly the older generation
of activists within our Polish American organizations, take offense when
such observations are presented. When, for example, at the last convention of the American Council of Polish Cultural Clubs, held at Du-
quesne University, in Pittsburgh, Mr. Stefan Jodlowski, an Instructor at
the Pennsylvania State University, compared the percentage of students
going on to college from three schools, one predominantly Jewish, one
predominantly Negro, and one predominantly Polish, and reported that
proportionately more Jews and Negroes go on to college than do Polish
Americans, the audience reacted in an hostile and emotional way to the
conclusions reached. And yet, on the basis of observations made by
college and university personnel to whom I have spoken, more Negroes
do go on to college than do Polish Americans. The United Negro College
Fund supports thirty-six colleges, 98.6% of whose 42,000 students are
Negro. By comparison, the Polish American Community supports Alliance College, with a total enrollment of six hundred, only 60% of whom are
of Polish American background, and St. Mary's College, at Orchard Lake,
which has a total enrollment of only one hundred and thirty. At two of
the three major colleges run by our Polish American teaching nuns, Holy
Family College, in Philadelphia, Villa Maria College, in Buffalo, and
Madonna College, in Livonia, Michigan, each of which services a major
Polish American Community, less than ten percent of the student body is
of Polish background.

Perhaps additional support for the observation that more Negroes go to college than do Polish Americans can be found in the greater cultural impact Negro Americans have made on America than have Polish Americans. One need only walk through any bookstore and count the number of works by Negroes and about Negroes and compare them to works by or about Poles and Polish Americans. So small is the interest in things Polish, even among Polish Americans, that publishers will often refuse to publish a book on a Polish subject unless it is subsidized. Though the average Negro American is not as well off financially as is his Polish American counterpart, he does take a greater interest in his heritage. An example of the interest students of Polish background take in their heritage can be seen in a nation-wide contest sponsored by The Kosciuszko Foundation to commemorate Poland's Millennium. It was open to all Americans attending accredited colleges and universities and offered a $1,000.00 six week tour of Europe and Poland as a first prize for any term paper on a Polish subject. Instead of writing a term paper on Napoleon or Bismarck for a course in Modern European History, to choose but one of many possibilities, all the student had to do was to write on any Pole of his choosing. In most instances he had to write a term paper for his course anyway. Yet not one entry was submitted by any student at Alliance College, St. Mary's College or by any student attending an institution of higher learning run by any of our Polish teaching orders. At Alliance there are no courses on Polish Music, Folklore or Art. There is no course on the History, Sociology, Economy, Psychology or Culture of Polish Americans. Nor has any significant attempt been made in quite some time to recruit recognized authorities in the Polish language, literature or history, at least not until Dr. Parcinski's present administration. The record at the schools run by our Polish religious orders is even worse. At St. Francis High School, in Athol Springs, New York, from which weekly appeals for funds from Polonia are broadcast over Father Justin's Rosary Hour, no courses in Polish language, history or culture are offered. And though a listing of extracurricular activities available for students includes a Stamp Club, a Chess Club and a French Club, we find no reference to a Polish Club.

Not merely does the Polish American Community provide little assistance or encouragement for its younger generation to learn of its heritage, often it works in the opposite direction. The following Letter to the Editor from Miss Marilyn Dwyer appeared in the November 21, 1967 issue of Dziennik Polski, under the title "Writer Bemoans Polonia Apathy." It is typical of what many Polish Americans must undergo:

By virtue of often being a guest at the home of my aunt in Hamtramck, I occassionally have the opportunity to see your paper. With great difficulty, I am able to get the gist of most of your headlines, and what I don't know myself, my aunt translates for me.

Recently the subject of one of our dinner-table discussions was the apathy of ''Polonia,'' and the lack of interest displayed by many young people in their ancestral heritage.

It is true that some young people will never appreciate their ethnic and cultural backgrounds, for they are primarily interested in material gains, rapid anglo-saxonization and the like.

However, there are others who do possess an interest or at least a potential interest in their cultural heritage, but are not given the opportunities to bring it to fruition. And it must be stressed that a grave offender in this area is "Polania" itself.

I am a product of a traditional Polish-American, Roman-Catholic educational experience. Eight years of Felician elementary school -- four years at one of Hamtramck's "Polish" high schools, and two years at a suburban Detroit all-girl college also run by the Felecian order.

I was one of those who has always displayed a marked interest in my ethnic background. However, throughout my educational experience I have known nothing but disappointment and frustration in this regard. Consistently the pastors, sisters superior, teaching nuns and others have, knowingly or not, stifled any initiative and creative interest in this area.

Individual teachers stressed the lack of a future for serious studies in Polish or simply refused aid and advice for a purported lack of time. And in the few instances when good intentions were indeed present, the individuals in question had no background or academic experience to offer any constructive and meaningful suggestions.

Although we tend often to speak about "Polish jokes" and the general disrepute in which American society in general supposedly holds the Polish American community, in my own case it was only there that my latent interest in the Polish area was given a substantial boost.

At the University of Michigan in Ann Arbor for the first time my serious intentions in this field were not treated as something second rate, and it was primarily persons with non-Polish backgrounds, that gave me the most substantive advice and encouragement.

I am now working on the revolutionary movements in Poland in the late 19th and early 20th centuries. I am presently dealing with such movements as the Social Democracy in Poland and Lithuania as well as with such personalities as Dzierzynski, Warynski and others.

But it was only through great individual perserverance and the aid of American professors and institutions that I was able to achieve my goal. In this respect "Polania" not only didn't help, but was actually a hindrance, which may have succeeded in discouraging a less resolute person than myself.

In reading Miss Dwyer's letter, I cannot help recalling the difficulties Dr. Stephen P. Mizwa had when attempting to establish The Kosciuszko Foundation some forty odd years ago; the institution which has done more than any other to promote an awareness of the need for higher education among Americans of Polish background, to assist our needy and deserving Polish American youth through meaningful scholarships, to develop a pride of heritage among Polish Americans and to acquaint our fellow Americans with Poland's cultural heritage through the publication

of books and cultural programs of a national scope. After appealing to
Polonia time and again, his only meaningful support came from non-Poles.
Among the seven original trustees of the Foundation, only Dr. Mizwa was
of Polish background. For many years the bulk of Polonia was unaware
of the need for such an institution.

Miss Dwyer's experience is typical. My own is similar. My
parish was founded in 1918. When I went on from college to graduate
school, in 1952, the first person in my parish to go beyond college, one
of our clergy told my mother: "Mrs. Kusielewicz, you are to be con-
gratulated on sending your son through college. But don't you think
you are making a mistake by sending him to graduate school? No one
in our parish has gone to graduate school. Do you want your son to
become a freak?" The clergyman was well intentioned, a virtuous priest
who believed he had the best interests of his flock at heart.

Most of the heads of our religious schools pay lip-service to their
Polish heritage whenever fund drives are underway. But few of them
deliver in the classroom. When speaking to responsible members of our
religious orders, I am told, more often than not, that there is no interest
in Polish language, history or culture among the Polish Americans in their
student body. Often, I have been told that there is no practical purpose
served in studying one's ethnic heritage or simply that "the sooner we
become American, the better." Somehow these educators are unaware
that persons are better Americans by knowing the path along which they
came. Somehow, these educators have failed to recognize the possibili-
ties of "motivation" in stimulating the interest of their students in their
Polish heritage. If a study were made, I feel confident that it would show
that the majority of those in our Polish American teaching orders suffer
from the same feeling of inferiority that is characteristic of the greater
part of the Polish American Community. Given the disgraceful, though
at times unconscious, way in which the American hierarchy has treated
Polonia, this feeling of inferiority is quite understandable among our
religious.

Though the history of the Poles in America dates back to 1608, the
year after the first permanent English settlement was established on the
shores of the United States, the greater part of what we call Polonia came
to America during the period from 1890-1914. Coming from the partitioned pieces of Poland, where Polish cultural and educational achievements were denied or ignored, these immigrants had little knowledge of
their own heritage, aside of a rudimentary knowledge of the Polish language,
strong religious beliefs that were based more on superstition than understanding and a knowledge of the traditions of their village, which they
tried to preserve here, a symbol of security and belonging in an otherwise
hostile world. They were good people, hard working, honest and sincere.
Their word was their bond, to such a degree that once they were established in America, they normally experienced no difficulties in obtaining
mortgages for their homes, generally being considered good risks. But
by and large, they were illiterate; with the exception of Prussia, neither
of the two remaining partitioning powers were committed to educating

their own people, let alone their Polish subjects; and even in Prussia, what little education was available for Poles was German.

Coming from agricultural backgrounds, the greater part of this Polish immigration lacked the skills necessary for survival in their new environments. Being generally illiterate, too proud to accept assistance from others and with few of their own to help them, that they survived at all is quite remarkable. The poorest Negroes migrating into the center cities had advantages the early Polish immigrants never possessed, for the Negroes at least understood the English language, and in many instances even looked down with contempt upon the "hunkie" newcomers. . . .

For all the shortcomings of their peasant environments, these Polish immigrants were aware of the importance of literacy and education. Soon after their arrival here, they established their own educational system, soon to number over five hundred schools, a remarkable phenomenon, when one considers that such a system did not exist even in the partitioned pieces of their fatherland.

Brought up in this environment, the next generation of Polish Americans was not content with simply an elementary education. Just as their parents were not content with their own educational experiences and went on to build their elementary school system, they sought secondary education. And though a number of high schools were built within the framework of the Polish American educational system, the costs involved made it impossible to construct a secondary system as complete as the primary system already in existence. More and more Polish Americans of this second generation went to the hostile environment of the public high schools, where things Polish were generally ignored or distorted, often reflecting the attitude of the partitioning powers towards Poland.

We must remember that the time the Poles were immigrating to the United States in large numbers, Americans began going to Europe in ever increasing numbers to study at the recently organized German graduate schools, especially in the field of history, in which German scholars were responsible for so many major contributions. When these students returned to America, their view of the world, and particularly of Eastern Europe, was German. As a result of the Anglo-Saxon racist attitudes they brought back with them, things Polish -- more generally things Eastern and Southern European -- were generally ignored in the text books they wrote, or they were presented in a negative way. Why, for example, these text books would ask, was Poland partitioned? "Because the Poles were incapable of governing themselves!" the old Prussian explanation that attempted to justify "the greatest crime in history." We might note here that this situation still exists.

Though Poles were among the first to arrive in America, though they helped to establish the first industries here, and though they fought the first successful strike for civil liberties in our history, in 1619, no mention of these facts appear in the text books used in our schools. In this regard, the Negro community is performing a great service for all minority groups, by insisting that their contributions be included in the texts and courses of our schools.

Not merely were things Polish ignored or distorted in the schools, but this second generation of Polish Americans was distinctly told that to be foreign was bad. The whole emphasis in the American educational system, just as in the Catholic Church, was to Americanize as quickly as possible, to melt all groups in the American pot. Not merely did this generation learn that to be foreign was bad, but it also became aware of the stereotypes Americans had of Polish Americans, the same stereotypes Americans still hold.

In a survey taken a few years ago by Wieslaw Kuniczak, author of The Thousand Hour Day and winner of a Book of the Month Club Award, Polish Americans were found to be "anti-Semite, narrow, simpleminded, clumsy, stupid, uninspired, ignorant, anti-liberal, reactionary, big, poor, vulgar, loud, peasant, drunk." In addition, this stereotype includes "Catholic, feudal, tough, honest -- but with the implication that Poles were too stupid to steal -- brave -- but with the implication that Poles lacked the imagination to be cautious -- angry, dull and so on. Seventeen said simply: Anti-Semetic. One said: Ugh!"

One need not read Kuniczak's The Silent Immigration to learn of these stereotypes. All one need do is to look at American television: the Carol Burnet Show, the Rowan and Martin Laugh In, etc. The reaction of many educated Polish Americans to these stereotypes and to these programs is to shrug them off or to ignore them, yet these programs reach tens of millions of persons across the country. It is interesting to note that Mr. Kuniczak's speech The Silent Immigration, like Mr. Jodlowski's study of the Jews, Negroes, and Poles going on to college, raised such a storm of protest within the Polish American Community, that it was among the factors responsible for his being denied a position as Writer in Residence at a leading Polish American College, where he could have done so much good encouraging young Polish Americans to become writers, a field in which the Polish American Community is almost completely unrepresented, and teaching them the most effective ways of breaking into this field.

Given the hostile climate in the public schools, the stereotypes and a failure to appreciate the achievements of their parents, especially when compared to the accomplishments of these living in the fashionable sections of town, usually on the other side of the tracks, it is not surprising that this second generation began turning away from its Polish heritage and developing a feeling of inferiority, especially after 1945, when at almost every Third of May rally, even their own Polish American leaders began condemning Poland as being Communist, often without considering the causes of this condition or differentiating between the government and the people.

One could expect that the Catholic Church -- the institution into which the Polish Americans poured their limited funds by the billions of dollars and to which they gave their greatest loyalty and support, identifying Pole as one and inseparable from Catholic -- would have attempted to stem this condition. Indeed, the Polish clergy achieved wonders in the early years, not merely in helping to preserve something of Polish customs and traditions, but also in creating small islands in which Polish Americans could find warmth and understanding in an otherwise hostile American environment. Unfortunately, the American hierarchy did not appreciate the needs of these immigrants, confident in the belief that the best way to serve them was to Americanize them as quickly as possible. Somehow, this hierarchy still does not realize that within the Polish American community, where Polish and Catholic are almost one and inseparable, to undermine the Polishness of this community was also to undermine its Catholicity. Nor has the American hierarchy ever appreciated the tremendous achievement of these immigrants, priests, brothers, nuns and laymen, whose contribution to the growth of the Catholic Church in America is wholly out of proportion to their numbers.

Those clergy who defended the interests of their community came under the displeasure of the "Irish" Church. In city after city across America we have outstanding churchmen who are continually ignored when appointments to bishoprics are made, simply because they served their people and their Church too well. Young Polish American seminarians and young Polish American priests came to look upon their Polish origins as a handicap which destines them in the eyes of the Irish hierarchy to the poorer areas in which the Polish parishes are found, which limits their opportunities to go on to the North American College in Rome or on to higher office in the Church. One need only look at the statistics to learn of the flagrant discrimination which the hierarchy of our "One, Holy, Irish and Apostolic Church" directs against the Polish American Community.

At least one out of eight, and perhaps as many as one out of six Catholics in the United States are of Polish background. According to the 1968 Catholic Directory there were 267 Cardinals, Archbishops and Bishops in the Catholic Church in America. One would therefore expect that approximately one out of eight or approximately 33 of these princes of the Church would be of Polish background. There are not 33, there are not 30, there are not 20, there are not even 10 bishops of Polish background in the American Church. As of the present moment there are only eight. Negro Americans would term this discrimination of the worst sort. The Polish American Community suffers this indignity in silence. During the Polish Millenium Celebrations, when I presented these statistics and the conclusions one may draw from them at a Millennium banquet attended by the local bishop, a delegation of Polish American clergy went some days later to apologize to the bishop for my affrontery.

Is it any wonder, then, that our young clergy of Polish American background look upon their Polishness as a liability and that they reflect this view in the administration of their parishes and of the schools attached to them? Is it not inevitable that this attitude will sooner or later be reflected in their parishionners as well?

Even those of our younger clergy who would wish to correct this situation experience difficulty. Few are permitted to go to the Polish Seminary at Orchard Lake to pursue their studies, even by the few Polish bishops in the Catholic Church. As few of these clergy read Polish, few are able to learn of Poland's contributions to the Church. Until now, we do not have scholarly biographies of the Polish saints after whom so many of our Polish American parishes are named; nor do we have any scholarly description in English of the Polish contribution to the development of Catholicism, or to the growth of the Catholic Church in the United States. Is it any wonder, then, that in Msgr. John Tracy Ellis' American Catholicism, the only reference to the Polish contribution to the Church in the United States is the schism caused when the Polish National Catholic Church was formed? Nor do we have an adequate account of the establishment of the Polish National Catholic Church, which fifty years ago foreshadowed the changes currently taking place within the Church.

Is it any wonder, then, that the Polish language, history and culture are so little taught in our Polish parochial schools or in schools run by our Polish religious orders? Is it any wonder, then, that the members of these orders fail to motivate their students to develop an interest in these subjects?

I have spent some time describing conditions within the Catholic Church, for the Polish parish still remains the core of the Polish American Community. If we cannot bring about changes here, then it will be almost impossible to bring about any truly effective changes in Polonia. If my observations are critical, I hope they are interpreted in a positive sense. I could not harm the institution with which I have been associated throughout the whole of my life: eight years at a Holy Family elementary school, four years at a Christian Brothers' high school, four years at a Vincentian college, three years and a doctorate from a Jesuit university and fourteen years on the staff of a Catholic university. However, I do feel an obligation to draw the attention of my listeners to a serious condition which an unresponsive hierarchy has in large part been responsible for.

One could likewise have expected our Polish organizations, particularly our Polish fraternal organizations -- which together with the Polish parishes form the pillars upon which the Polish American Community rests -- to combat the conditions that bring about this feeling of inferiority. Indeed, for many years our Fraternals were in the forefront of Polonia's cultural life.

The Polish National Alliance of the United States, recognizing the need for higher education for Polish Americans, established Alliance College. The Polish Roman Catholic Union established the Museum and Archives of the Polish Roman Catholic Union. In their early years, our fraternals made a good beginning in the field of publications, not merely in the area of newspapers, but also in that of books. But all of these were in Polish. For a while the Polish Roman Catholic Union began to step in

the right direction when it published the Annals that were edited by Mie-
ceslas Haiman. But in recent years almost nothing is being done. As
late as seven years ago, Alliance College deteriorated to such a condition
that only the threat of having its accreditation removed could motivate
the directors of the Polish National Alliance to a renewed interest in the
school. In recent years, too, the condition of the Museum and Archives
of the Polish Roman Catholic Union has deteriorated drastically. Similar conditions are reflected in most of our other fraternals.

All too often those who are directing these institutions are blamed
for conditions over which they have no control and which they are trying,
often heroically, to stem. Often our fraternals are criticized for failing
to include representatives of the third generation of Polish Americans
among their responsible officials -- that generation which went beyond the
elementary school outlook of the second generation, to a wider university
outlook, together with everything this connotes. Unfortunately, this third
generation also suffers from the same feeling of inferiority that is characteristic of the rest of Polonia. True, there are indications of a greater
interest in its Polish heritage among the members of this generation, but
there are few places in which this third generation can learn of that heritage, as Miss Dwyer's experience, quoted earlier in this paper, illustrates. As few of those members of this third generation who have gone
on to university studies have taken part in the activities of the fraternals,
our fraternals, like most of the other organizations within the Polish
American Community, have not significantly advanced over the achievements of the second generation of Polish Americans.

Had this generation gap not taken place, I am confident the conditions
to which Alliance College, the Museum and Archives of the Polish Roman
Catholic Union and the cultural and political life of Polonia as a whole would
never have deteriorated to the extent they did.

But the gap did occur. And it is reflected in all the aspects of
Polonia's life, especially in its lack of sophistication and professionalism.
An example of this lack of sophistication and professionalism is to be
seen in the commemoration of the landing of the Poles at Jamestown, in
1958. When the Polish American Congress decided to commemorate this
event with the publication of The Poles at Jamestown, they approached
the problem as it would have been approached thirty years ago, by going
to one of the few college graduates they knew: perhaps the local pastor,
the principal of a parochial school, or to a local writer for a Polish
newspaper. Lacking the sophistication, the awareness that the university educated third generation could give, professional historians were
ignored. The result, if Philip Barbour's review of The Poles at Jamestown, published in the William and Mary Quarterly, is to serve as a criterion, was embarassing to Polonia, to say the least.

Another example of this lack of professionalism is to be seen in the
quality of the many books and pamphlets that were published by Polonia to
commemorate the Polish Millennium. With the exception of those published
by The Kosciuszko Foundation, these books and pamphlets were even less
professionally done than The Poles at Jamestown, even when over $30,000.00

was spent on one such publication. A negatively inclined sociologist or cultural historian could have a field day if he used these publications as a basis on which to approach the cultural development of Polonia.

This lack of professionalism -- this lack of advancement over the achievements of the second generation -- is likewise to be seen in the scholarship programs of our Polish organizations. At a time when educators hold that scholarships of less than $500.00 are meaningless, aside of some incentive value, and when more and more are beginning to question the value of scholarships of less than $1,000.00, the greatest part of scholarships given by Polish American organizations are still under $100.00. Furthermore, with the exception of The Kosciuszko Foundation, I know of no Polish organization that seeks to obtain matching funds for the scholarships they give from the colleges or universities which their grantees are attending; nor, again with the exception of the scholarships granted by The Kosciuszko Foundation, is there any attempt to utilize the scholarships granted to encourage Polish Americans to go on for degrees in Polish Studies or into fields in which the Polish American Community is under-represented: government service, the arts, and the mass media.

We mentioned earlier that there is a greater interest on the part of our third generation in its Polish heritage. But like Miss Dwyer, this generation faces all sorts of difficulties. Not merely the hindrance and discouragement of Polonia, but also the lack of sources in which it can learn of its heritage. This younger generation does not read Polish. If it is to learn of its heritage, it must do so through books published in English. Yet these books do not exist.

We are proud of the Polish tradition of tolerance. Yet there is no book in the English language that tells of this tradition. Is it difficult to understand, then, why Kuniczak finds Americans looking upon Poles as "narrow"? Poland has made contributions to the development of representative government. Yet there is no easily available book in English that tells of this contribution. Is it difficult to understand, then, why Kuniczak finds Americans looking upon Poles as "reactionary" or "anti-liberal"? Not merely did more Poles lose their lives assisting their Jewish neighbors during World War II then did any other people, but in few countries of the world did the Jews have a freer opportunity of development than they had in Poland. Yet there is no book in English that tells this story. Is it difficult to understand, then, why Kuniczak finds Americans looking upon Poles as "anti-Semites"? There are, as we have already read, no scholarly biographies of our Polish saints, nor any history of Poland's contributions to the Catholic Church. Is it therefore surprising that our Polish American clergy have so much difficulty in securing recognition? Nor do we have adequate treatments of Polish contributions to music, art, folklore, the dance, etc. Nor do any of our Polish American institutions of higher learning have any course in these fields. How then, is this third generation, which is desperately needed to give our Polish American organizations the new life they need, to overcome its feeling of inadequacy and to develop that sense of pride that is the first step to participation?

I have dwelt for some time upon the historical development of Polonia and on conditions as I believe them to exist today, for it is only through such an approach that I believe we can make some recommendations that would be effective in solving the problems we face. And this, not out of a desire to stimulate Polish patriotism, but in an attempt to face our responsibilities as Americans. For each of us is a better American by understanding his roots: the traditions, accomplishments and faults of his ancestors.

As scholars, intellectuals and educators, we live in a world that often has little bearing with the masses of Polonia, in which we are accepted on the basis of our contributions to society. We are not affected by the jibes, the jokes, the discriminations leveled against the masses of our people in the same way as they. However, we do have a responsibility to them.

It is unfortunate that my study is based primarily on observation; not upon the sort of detailed scholarly studies an historian or a sociologist would prefer. Unfortunately, the study of Polonia has been neglected. Unfortunately we do not have such studies on a scale that would approach the magnitude of problems before us. Nevertheless, we must begin somewhere, if only with personal observations.

DETROIT'S BLACK-POLISH CONFERENCE: "A STATE-

MENT OF PURPOSE"

1969

During the late 1960's Americans became increasingly
conscious of the problems of their cities -- decaying
neighborhoods, the flight of the middle class to the
suburbs, a declining tax base, inadequate social services,
polarization between the races. The Black-Polish Conference of Detroit tried to minimize the negative
consequences of racial difference in a city where these
two "minorities" were indeed the real majority.

Two out of every three Detroiters is either Black or Polish. Their
predominance in the Detroit community should result in a great deal of
interaction between the two groups. The Black and Polish communities
often share the same neighborhoods, schools, and places of employment.
This daily contact results in their sharing many of the same problems and
goals.

Our basic premise is that each community would be greatly aided in
dealing with these common problems and goals if they worked more closely
together. The Black-Polish Conference of Greater Detroit is, therefore,
established for the following purposes:

To promote increased knowledge of the history and culture of each
community by the other through public meetings and cultural and educational programs;

To develop and expand the channels of communication between the two
groups, particularly on matters of current community concern, not only
between the leadership, but also between the individuals in each community;
and,

To sponsor specific programs of mutual benefit to the Black and
Polish communities.

A YOUNG POLISH AMERICAN SPEAKS UP: "THE MYTH OF THE

MELTING POT"

1970

Barbara Mikulski's statement at a meeting of the Task
Force on Urban Problems of the United States Catholic
Conference made the point briefly and pungently that all
was not well with the ethnic American who often also was
a working class American.

America is not a melting pot. It is a sizzling cauldron for the ethnic
American who feels that he has been politically extorted by both government and private enterprise. The ethnic American is sick of being stereo-
typed as a racist and dullard by phoney white liberals, pseudo black mili-
tants and patronizing bureaucrats. He pays the bill for every major
government program and gets nothing or little in the way of return. Tricked
by the political rhetoric of the illusionary funding for black-oriented
social programs, he turns his anger to race--when he himself is the
victim of class prejudice. He has worked hard all of his life to become
a "good American;" he and his sons have fought on every battlefield -- then
he is made fun of because he likes the flag.

The Ethnic American is overtaxed and underserved at every level
of government. He does not have fancy lawyers or expensive lobbyists
getting him tax breaks on his income. Being a home owner he shoulders
the rising property taxes -- the major revenue source for the municipalities
in which he lives. Yet he enjoys very little from these unfair and bur-
densome levies. Because of restrictive eligibility requirements linked
either to income or "target areas," he gets no help from Federal programs.
If he wants to buy in the "old neighborhood" he cannot get an FHA loan.
One major illness in his family will wipe him out. When he needs a nurs-
ing home for an elderly parent, he finds that there are none that he can
afford nor is he eligible for any financial assistance. His children tend
to go to parochial schools which receive little in the way of government
aid and for which he carries an extra burden. There is a general decline
of community services for his neighborhood, e. g., zoning, libraries, recreation programs, sanitation, etc.

His income of $5,000 to $10,000 per year makes him "near poor."
He is the guy that is hurt by layoffs, tight money that chokes him with high
interest rates for installment buying and home improvements. Manu-
facturers with their price fixing, shoddy merchandise and exorbitant
repair bills are gouging him to death. When he complains about costs, he
is told that it is the "high cost of labor" that is to blame. Yet he knows
he is the "labor" and that in terms of real dollars he is going backwards.

The ethnic American also feels unappreciated for the contribution
he makes to society. He resents the way the working-class is looked
down upon. In many instances he is treated like the machine he operates

or the pencil he pushes. He is tired of being treated like an object of production. The public and private institutions have made him frustrated by their lack of response to his needs. At present he feels powerless in his daily dealings with and efforts to change them.

Unfortunately, because of old prejudices and new fears, anger is generated against other minority groups rather than those who have power. What is needed is an alliance of white and black; white collar, blue collar, and no collar based on mutual need, interdependence and respect, an alliance to develop the strategy for a new kind of community organization and political participation.

THE MEANING OF THE 3RD OF MAY IN 1972: "A REVOLUTION

IN REVERSE"

1972

> Speaking in the apparently more conservative atmosphere
> of 1972, Aloysius Mazewski, president of the Polish
> American Congress, saw yet another meaning in one of
> the landmarks of Polish history. His remarks were
> delivered to the Indiana Division of the Congress at a
> religious memorial observance of the Polish Constitution
> of May 3, 1791.

I feel it would be redundant to describe to you events and persons
that made the May 3rd, 1791 Constitution of the old Royal Republic of
Poland possible. As an intelligent audience, you know the Polish history,
and you have heard and appraised its highlights on many other occasions
in the past.

[A brief review of the constitution's significance in 1791 follows.]

It is, however, not sufficient for our historical values and directions,
to merely commemorate the event that gave Poland the May 3rd Constitution.

We pay homage to the authors of this great and noble document by
praising the nobility of their pursuits and purposes, their sense of justice,
their deep and abiding feeling for Poland's destiny.

And, noble, as these sentiments are, they are not, in themselves, a
sufficient homage to those great men. I do not think they expected our
praise. But I firmly believe that they expected the generations of Poles
that followed them to be faithful, even unto the death, to the ideals they
incorporated in the May 3rd Constitution.

It is proper and fitting that we revere their names.

But to pay really meaningful and substantive tribute to their great-
ness, we must apply the enduring relevancy of their work to the problems
and challenges of our times.

In this context and this frame of reference, the May 3rd Constitution has a deep meaning and vital message not only to Poles. It has a
universal appeal to all men who know the meaning and value of freedom
and dignity of man.

It has an extraordinary relevancy to the problems and crisis of the
United States of today.

It has a great lesson for the present generations of Americans.

And having these attributes, the May 3rd Constitution is truly a
universal document in the annals of mankind.

It is one of the great contributions Poland made to the inception,
growth and development of political and civic precepts of the Western man.

What, then is the May 3rd Constitution relevancy to our contemporary
America?

Appraising it from the distance of almost two hundred years, and from the American point of view, we discover one inescapable fact, unique in the history of man.

Namely -- that the May 3rd Constitution was a revolutionary document, but it embodies a revolution in reverse.

All other revolutions in the history of man were revolutions against individual tyrannies of kings and magnates, against brutal injustices, against dehumanization of the common man.

Poland's revolution was of an entirely different type.

The 18th Century Poland was the most liberal state in Europe.

While, for instance, in England at that time only about four percent of the population enjoyed enfranchisement, in Poland more than twelve percent of the population had the right to legislate at Sejmiki, at the Sejm, and the right to elect the King.

In addition to that, the spirit of tolerance was prevalent.

As a matter of fact, Poland was enjoying too much freedom for the political atmosphere and customs of the past centuries.

Thus, May 3rd Constitution, putting restrictions on freedom grown wild and irresponsible, was a revolution in reverse.

It was a revolution against too much permissiveness, too much irresponsibility in civic matters, too much demand upon the state without commensurate contributions to the welfare and viability of the state.

A situation similar to that which afflicted the 18th Century Poland, is prevailing in the United States today. It has modern trappings, but essentially does not differ from the freedom gone wild, the permissiveness, the disregard for public good that brought Poland once the most powerful state in Europe, to the brink of dissolution and anarchy.

The ill-fated Polish Liberum Veto, the political irresponsibility of the gentry, its frivolous statements that Poland stands on misrule -- "Polska nierzadem stoi" -- all these national afflictions and sin find their equivalent in our America of today.

Excessive permissiveness is bringing chaos to our moral precepts and rules. Irresponsibility toward the state is evident in anti-war demonstrations, in draft card burning, in insecurity on our streets, in devaluation of American spirit in our universities and colleges where teaching and scientific discipline is being replaced by the absurdity of students' demands and the meek accession to these demands by the faculty.

The vast cultural wasteland named television is distracting our mental and intellectual powers from real problems to showing of presentation more fitted for circuses than for enlightened public.

Hedonism, the fanatical pursuits of personal pleasures and satisfactions has its reflection in the pre-May 3rd Poland, . . .

Poland paid dearly for these mistakes. The renascence of the May 3rd Constitution came too late to save the 18th century generations of Poles.

Poland paid for these sins with blood and sweat, sacrifices, heroism and exiles of her best sons.

And those who died during the Kosciuszko Resurrection, during the Napoleonic wars, during the November [and] January uprisings, in two world wars,--they made both the expiation and the down payment for the future of Poland. That future in freedom, justice and self determination is not yet in sight for our generations of Poles.

But the knowledge of the May 3rd Constitution, and its message emblazoned in the hearts of whole generations of Poles, not only sustain us in these times of trials and tribulations, but instill in our hearts unshakeable conviction that some day Poland will take its rightful place among the free and independent nations of the world.

And what is the message of May 3rd Constitution to us, as Poles living in the United States and as Americans of Polish origin and ancestry?

Directly to us, the May 3rd Constitution speaks that the fullness of life lies primarily in patriotic living.

To understand our land and the needs and aspirations of our people;

To participate in the solution of crisis and responses to challenges;

To observe the law of the land as the safeguard of peace, security and viable society;

And to instill in the hearts and minds of our children both the love for our land and respect for its institutions of freedom, together with a deeply ingrained sense of social and national responsibilities,--

These are the duties and obligations which the meaning of May 3rd Constitution places upon us.

And when we leave this place and this program with renewed determination and commitment to a more patriotic living, then our observance will be blessed, indeed.

And the May 3rd Constitution Observance each year will enrich the substance of our lives as Poles and Americans of Polish heritage.

APPENDICES

APPENDIX I

POLISH AMERICAN POPULATION BY STATES: 1910, 1960
(Sources: United States Census, 1910, 1960)

Division and State	1910			1960		
	Total Polish Stock	Foreign Born Poles	Native of Polish Parent(s)	Total Polish Stock	Foreign Born Poles	Native of Polish Parent(s)
United States	1,707,640	943,781	763,859	2,780,026	581,936	2,198,090
New England:	163,015	108,073	54,942	284,316	67,303	217,013
Maine	2,037	1,533	504	3,092	635	2,457
New Hampshire	5,262	3,733	1,531	7,649	1,843	5,806
Vermont	2,684	2,025	659	3,004	604	2,400
Massachusetts	87,006	58,273	28,273	136,942	33,199	103,743
Rhode Island	10,678	7,037	3,641	15,966	3,683	12,283
Connecticut	55,356	35,472	19,874	117,663	27,336	90,327
Middle Atlantic:	713,588	427,224	286,364	1,222,254	248,580	973,674
New York	283,733	168,841	114,892	683,610	139,591	544,019
New Jersey	107,657	70,107	37,550	238,532	53,448	185,084
Pennsylvania	322,198	188,276	133,922	300,112	55,541	244,571
East North Central:	643,003	318,863	324,140	895,031	200,041	694,990
Ohio	78,084	41,828	36,256	143,165	28,833	114,165
Indiana	29,121	14,530	14,591	43,820	9,350	34,470
Illinois	274,661	148,809	125,852	358,916	87,154	271,762
Michigan	132,222	62,606	69,616	255,467	58,061	197,406
Wisconsin	128,915	51,090	77,825	93,663	16,643	77,020

Division and State	1910			1960		
	Total Polish Stock	Foreign Born Poles	Native of Polish Parent(s)	Total Polish Stock	Foreign Born Poles	Native of Polish Parent(s)
West North Central:	95,632	41,148	54,484	77,972	12,489	65,483
Minnesota	49,142	20,153	28,989	33,659	5,358	28,301
Iowa	4,314	2,156	2,158	4,213	910	3,303
Missouri	16,328	8,444	7,884	19,856	3,525	16,331
North Dakota	4,794	1,850	2,944	2,823	299	2,524
South Dakota	2,399	765	1,634	1,532	149	1,383
Nebraska	13,648	5,166	8,482	10,679	1,565	9,114
Kansas	5,007	2,614	2,393	5,210	683	4,527
South Atlantic:	43,572	24,592	18,980	115,540	20,705	94,835
Delaware	6,189	3,657	2,532	8,105	1,410	6,695
Maryland	24,784	12,924	11,860	39,906	6,023	33,883
Dist. of Columbia	1,120	568	552	5,667	1,179	4,488
Virginia	2,620	1,437	1,183	8,845	1,045	7,800
West Virginia	7,018	5,126	1,892	8,308	1,892	6,416
North Carolina	268	113	155	2,756	470	2,286
South Carolina	490	233	257	2,038	204	1,834
Georgia	837	420	417	4,669	659	4,010
Florida	246	114	132	35,246	7,823	27,423
East South Central:	3,918	1,942	1,976	8,949	1,215	7,734
Kentucky	1,349	615	734	2,564	348	2,216
Tennessee	1,113	582	531	3,244	520	2,724
Alabama	951	520	431	2,226	246	1,980
Mississippi	505	225	280	915	101	814

Division and State	1910			1960		
	Total Polish Stock	Foreign Born Poles	Native of Polish Parent(s)	Total Polish Stock	Foreign Born Poles	Native of Polish Parent(s)
West South Central:	19,765	7,367	12,398	26,412	3,613	22,799
Arkansas	1,429	582	847	1,112	187	925
Louisiana	1,635	733	902	2,745	516	2,229
Oklahoma	3,007	1,301	1,706	3,072	415	2,657
Texas	13,694	4,751	8,943	19,483	2,495	16,988
Mountain:	9,178	5,695	3,483	21,324	3,671	17,653
Montana	2,147	1,325	822	2,346	433	1,913
Idaho	625	308	317	737	90	647
Wyoming	1,461	997	464	1,216	231	985
Colorado	3,990	2,498	1,492	7,323	1,355	5,968
New Mexico	264	133	131	1,336	126	1,210
Arizona	237	177	60	6,388	1,165	5,223
Utah	309	168	141	797	146	651
Nevada	145	89	56	1,181	125	1,156
Pacific:	15,969	8,877	7,092	128,228	24,319	103,909
Washington	6,523	3,780	2,743	11,172	2,067	9,105
Oregon	2,663	1,502	1,161	5,136	777	4,359
California	6,783	3,595	3,188	110,086	21,304	88,782
Alaska				891	91	740
Hawaii				1,003	80	923

N.B. The statistics in these tables are not strictly comparable from one year to the other. The totals for 1910 are based on the respondents' mother tongue. In 1960, total Polish stock refers to the country of origin (Poland, which was ethnically almost all Polish in 1960) and includes first and second generations. The foreign born Polish population is based on the mother tongue of the respondents, and the second generation (natives with one or both parents Polish) is determined by substracting the second figure from the first. The probability is very high that the federal census has always underestimated the Polish American population.

APPENDIX II

POLISH AMERICAN FRATERNALS

STATISTICS 1961, 1971

(Source: The Fraternal Monitor)

Fraternal	Year Founded		No. of Lodges	Insurance in force	Insurance written
Alliance of Poles in America 6966 Broadway Avenue Cleveland, Ohio	1895	1961	92	$10,831,316	$449,800 (1962)
		1971	79	12,940,144	429,700
Association of the Sons of Poland 665 Newark Avenue Jersey City, N.J.	1903	1961	116	9,970,551	320,900 (1962)
		1971	106	9,491,310	306,500
Polish Association of America 3068 South 13th St. Milwaukee, Wisconsin	1895	1961			
		1971	90	3,947,365	315,428
Polish Beneficial Association 2595 Orthodox St. Philadelphia, Pa.	1900	1962	126	11,767,051	415,628
		1971	113	10,900,596	286,950
Polish Falcons of America 97-99 So. 18th St. Pittsburgh, Pa.	1926	1962	184	13,180,695	1,122,750
		1971	168	16,410,991	1,136,242
Polish National Alliance 1514-20 W. Division Chicago, Illinois	1880	1961	1,494	277,838,277	12,493,083 (1962)
		1971	1,343	328,830,201	16,739,000
Polish National Alliance of Brooklyn, U.S.A. 155 Noble Street Brooklyn, N.Y.	1903	1961	229	15,131,504	722,800 (1962)
		1971	158	14,506,490	557,500
Polish National Union of America 1002 Pittston Avenue Scranton, Pa.	1908	1961	236	21,719,117	1,494,800 (1962)
		1971	229	29,409,059	2,133,300

Fraternal	Year Founded		No. of Lodges	Insurance in force	Insurance written
Polish Roman Catholic Union	1873	1961	990	$108,472,135	$3,568,860 (1962)
984 Milwaukee Avenue Chicago, Illinois		1971	903	110,010,440	3,979,500
Polish Union of America	1890	1961	145	10,677,259	267,706 (1962)
761 Fillmore Avenue Buffalo, New York		1971	129	10,759,775	576,500
Polish Union of the United States	1890	1961	358	12,419,436	296,250 (1962)
58-59 North Main St. Wilkes-Barre, Pa.		1971	300	11,479,881	472,500
Polish White Eagle Association	1906	1961	16	2,069,391	66,000 (1962)
1302 Second St., N.E. Minneapolis, Minn.		1971	15	2,465,899	84,000
Polish Women's Alliance of America	1898	1961	1,189	52,142,943	1,947,900 (1962)
1309-15 N. Ashland Chicago, Illinois		1971	1,046	58,095,412	1,936,000
Union of Polish Women in America	1921	1961	74	3,724,449	162,600 (1962)
2636-38 E. Allegheny Philadelphia, Pa.		1971	69	4,367,497	171,000
Totals: 14 fraternals	1873-1926	1961	5,249	549,944,124	23,329,077 (1962)
		1971	4,748	623,615,060	29,124,120

APPENDIX III

POLISH AMERICAN PUBLICATIONS

All of the following periodicals, except for academic journals, have a circulation of at least 2,000.

Polish American Newspapers

Dziennik Polski. 2310 Cass Avenue, Detroit, Michigan 48201. Pp. 6, daily; pp. 12, Sunday. Annual subscription: $28.00.

Dziennik Zwiazkowy. 1201 Milwaukee Avenue, Chicago, Illinois 60622. Pp. 8, daily; pp. 16, Sunday. Annual subscription: $26.00.

Nowy Dziennik. 253 Washington Street, Jersey City, New Jersey 17302. Pp. 16, daily; pp. 24, Sunday. Annual subscription: $26.00

Zwiazkowiec. 475 Queen Street, W., Toronto 156, Ontario, Canada. Pp. 8, daily. Annual subscription: $9.00; $10.00 outside Canada.

Polish Language Weeklies

Glos Ludowy. 5854 Chene Street, Detroit, Michigan 48211. Pp. 12. Annual subscription: $7.00.

Gwiazda Polarna. 3535 Jefferson Street, Stevens Point, Wisconsin 54481. Pp. 16. Annual subscription: $10.00.

Polonia. 1200 N. Ashland Avenue, #422, Chicago, Illinois 60622. Pp. 16. Annual subscription: $10.00.

Pittsburczanin. 3513-15 Butler Street, Pittsburgh, Pennsylvania 15201. Pp. 6. Annual subscription: $5.00.

Polish Monthly

Panorama. 1915 W. 9th Street, Los Angeles, California 90006.

English Language Weeklies

Am-Pol Eagle. 1335 E. Delavan Avenue, Buffalo, New York 14215. Pp. 16. Annual subscription: $6.50.

Post Eagle. 800 Van Houten Avenue, Clifton, New Jersey 07013. Pp. 16. Annual subscription: $5.00.

Polish Daily News. 2310 Cass Avenue, Detroit, Michigan 48201. Pp. 8. Annual subscription: $6.00.

Polish-English Weeklies

Czas. 142 Grand Street, Brooklyn, New York 11211. Pp. 8. Annual subscription: $1.50.

Gazeta Polonii. 610 Dorchester Avenue, South Boston, Massachusetts 02127. Pp. 12. Annual subscriptions: $7.00.

Gwiazda. 3022 Richmond Street, Philadelphia, Pennsylvania 19134. Pp. 6. Annual subscription: $6.00.

Polish-English Language Bi-weeklies

Kuryer Zjednoczenia. 6805 Lansing Avenue, Cleveland, Ohio 44105. Pp. 6. Annual subscriptions: $3.00.

Polish American Journal. 409 Cedar Avenue, Scranton, Pennsylvania 18505. Annual subscription: $3.00.

Zwiazkowiec. 6964 Broadway Avenue, Cleveland, Ohio 44106. Pp. 8. Annual subscription: $2.50.

Academic Journals

Polish American Studies. 984 Milwaukee Avenue, Chicago, Illinois 60622. Pp. 64. Semi-annual. Annual subscription: $5.00.

The Polish Review. 59 E. 66th Street, New York, New York 10021. Pp. 128. Quarterly. Annual subscription: $8.00.

Specialized Publications

Sodalis-Polonia. Orchard Lake Schools, Orchard Lake, Michigan 48033. Pp. 32. In Polish. Monthly. Annual subscription: $4.00.

Rola Boza. 529 E. Locust, Scranton, Pennsylvania 18505. Pp. 16. Polish and English. Monthly. Annual subscription: $5.00.

N.B. Adapted from a directory of Polish American publications published by the Orchard Lake Center for Polish Studies and Culture.

APPENDIX IV

POLISH AMERICAN CULTURAL INSTITUTIONS:

A SHORT LIST

Colleges

Alliance College, Cambridge Springs, Pennsylvania.

Felician College, Lodi, New Jersey.

Holy Family College, Philadelphia, Pennsylvania.

Madonna College, Livonia, Michigan.

Orchard Lake Schools (St. Mary's College, SS. Cyril and Methodius Seminary, Center for Polish Studies and Culture), Orchard Lake, Michigan.

Villa Maria College, Buffalo, Michigan.

Foundations and Research Centers

The Jurzykowski Foundation, New York City.

The Kosciuszko Foundation, New York City.

The Joseph Pilsudski of America, New York City.

The Polish Institute of Arts and Sciences, New York City.

The Polish Museum of America, Chicago, Illinois.

American Council of Polish Cultural Clubs

Krakowiak Polish Dancers, Boston, Massachusetts.

Polish Arts Club, Buffalo, New York.

Polish Club of Alliance College, Cambridge Springs, Pennsylvania.

Polish Arts Club, Chicago, Illinois.

Society of Polish Arts and Letters, Chicago, Illinois.

Friends of Polish Art, Detroit, Michigan.

Polish Heritage Society, Grand Rapids, Michigan.

Helena Modrzejewska Polish Cultural Club, Los Angeles, California.

Polanki, Milwaukee, Wisconsin.

Polanie Club, Minneapolis-St. Paul, Minnesota.

Polish Arts Club, Newark, New Jersey.

Club Polonaise, Passaic, New Jersey.

Polish Heritage Society, Philadelphia, Pennsylvania.

Polish Arts League, Pittsburgh, Pennsylvania.

Polish Arts Group, Rochester, New York.

Paderewski University Club, Scranton, Pennsylvania.

Chopin Fine Arts Club, South Bend, Indiana.

Polish Arts League, Syracuse, New York.

Polish American Arts Association, Washington, D. C.

Polish Arts Club, Youngstown, Ohio.

APPENDIX V

A BRIEF BIBLIOGRAPHY: BOOKS IN ENGLISH

Allswang, John M. A House for All Peoples: Ethnic Politics in Chicago 1890-1936. Lexington, Kentucky: The University Press of Kentucky, 1971.

Andrews, Theodore. The Polish National Catholic Church in America and Poland. London: S. P. C. K., 1953.

Bakanowski, Adolf. Polish Circuit Rider. Trans. and ed. Marion Moore Coleman. Cheshire, Connecticut: Cherry Hill Books, 1971. The memoirs of a Polish missionary in Texas during 1866-1870.

Balch, Emily G. Our Slavic Fellow Citizens. New York: Charities Publication Committee, 1910.

Cole, Donald B. Immigrant City: Lawrence, Massachusetts, 1845-1921. Chapel Hill, North Carolina: University of North Carolina Press, 1963.

Domanski, S. J., Francis, et al. The Contribution of the Poles to the Growth of Catholicism in the United States. Rome, 1959.

Fischer, Le Roy H. Lincoln's Gadfly, Adam Gurowski. Norman, Oklahoma: University of Oklahoma Press, 1964.

Fishman, Joshua A., et al. Language Loyalty in the United States: The Maintenance and Perpetuation of Non-English Mother Tongues by American Ethnic and Religious Groups. The Hague: Mouton and Company, 1966.

Fox, Paul. The Poles in America. New York: Arno, 1970. Reprint of the 1922 edition.

Gerson, Louis L. Woodrow Wilson and the Rebirth of Poland 1914-1920. New Haven: Yale University Press, 1953.

Gerson, Louis L. The Hyphenate in Recent American Politics and Diplomacy. Lawrence, Kansas: University of Kansas Press, 1964.

Greene, Victor. The Slavic Community on Strike: Immigrant Labor in Pennsylvania Anthracite. Notre Dame, Indiana: University of Notre Dame Press, 1968.

Halecki, Oscar. History of Poland. New York: Roy, 1956. A handy summary of Polish history, useful for putting the immigration into context.

Haiman, Miecislaus. Kosciuszko in the American Revolution. New York: Polish Institute of Arts and Sciences in America, 1943.

Haiman, Miecislaus. Kosciuszko, Leader and Exile. New York: Polish Institute of Arts and Sciences, 1946.

Haiman, Miecislaus. Polish Past in America, 1608-1865. Chicago: Polish Roman Catholic Union Archives and Museum, 1939.

Leslie, R. F. Polish Politics and the Revolution of November 1830. London: The Athlone Press, 1956. Useful for its discussion of the peasant question in Russian Poland in the early nineteenth century.

Lerski, Jerzy J. A Polish Chapter in Jacksonian America. Madison: University of Wisconsin Press, 1958. The Polish revolution of 1830 and the Great Emigration in American life and diplomacy during the 1830's.

Lubell, Samuel. The Future of American Politics. New York: Harper and Brothers, 1952.

Manning, Clarence A. Soldier of Liberty. Casimir Pulaski. New York: Philosophical Library, 1945.

Nesterowicz, Stefan. Travel Notes. Trans. and ed. Marion Moore Coleman. Chesire, Connecticut: Cherry Hill Books, 1968. A survey of Polish communities in the Middle West and Southwest in the early twentieth century.

Niemcewicz, Julian Urzyn. Under Their Vine and Fig Tree. Travels through America in 1797-1799, 1805 with some further Account of Life in New Jersey. Vol. XIV of The Collections of the New Jersey Historical Society. Elizabeth, N. J.: The Grassman Publishing Company, 1965.

Olszyk, Edmund. The Polish Press in America. Milwaukee: Marquette University Press, 1940.

Poles of Chicago 1837-1937. Chicago: Polish Pageant, Inc., 1937.

Theoharis, Athan G. The Yalta Myths: An Issue in U. S. Politics. Columbia, Missouri: University of Missouri Press, 1970.

Thomas, William I. and Znaniecki, Florian. The Polish Peasant in Europe and America. New York: Dover Publications, 1958. A reprint of the second, revised edition.

Turek, Victor, ed. The Polish Past in Canada. Toronto: Polish Research Institute in Canada, 1960.

Walker, Mack. Germany and the Emigration 1816-1885. Cambridge, Massachusetts: Harvard University Press, 1964. Sidelights on the emigration from the Polish provinces of Prussia.

Wepsiec, Jan. Polish American Serial Publications 1842-1966: An Annotated Bibliography. Chicago: Privately printed, 1968.

Wieczerzak, Joseph W. A Polish Chapter in Civil War America. New York: Twayne, 1967.

Wood, Arthur Evans. Hamtramck, Then and Now. A Sociological Study of a Polish American Community. New York: Bookman Associates, 1955.

Wytrwal, Joseph A. America's Polish Heritage. A Social History of the Poles in America. Detroit: Endurance Press, 1961.

Fiction

Algren, Nelson. Never Come Morning. New York: Harper and Brothers, 1942.

Algren, Nelson. The Neon Wilderness. Garden City, New York: Doubleday, 1947.

Algren, Nelson. The Man with the Golden Arm. Garden City, N. Y.: Doubleday, 1949.

Bankowsky, Richard. A Glass Rose. New York: Random House, 1958.

Bankowsky, Richard. After Penticost. New York: Random House, 1961.

Coleman, Marion Moore. A World Remembered. Tales and Lore of the Polish Land. Cheshire, Connecticut: Cherry Hill Books, 1965.

Gronowicz, Antoni. An Orange Full of Dreams. New York: Dodd, Mead, 1971.

Reymont, Wladyslaw. The Peasants. New York: Knopf, 1924-1925.

Sienkiewicz, Henryk. After Bread. New York: Fenno, 1897.

Sinclair, Upton. The Jungle. Several editions.

Tabrah, Ruth. Pulaski Place. New York: Harper and Brothers, 1949.

NAME INDEX

NAME INDEX

Adamowski, Benjamin, 33
Andrzejkowicz, Julius, 9

Bakanowski, Adolph, 6
Bankowsky, Richard, 32
Bardonski, Victor, 11
Barzynski, John, 7
Barzynski, Rev. John, 12
Barzynski, Vincent, 8,9,10,11
Biernacki-Poray, Wladek O., 34
Boyle, W.A. (Tony), 37
Bryan, William Jennings, 12
Buhaczkowski, Witold, 15

Cermak, Anton, 23
Churchill, Winston, 28
Coveleski, Stanley, 21

Dabrowski, Joseph, 8,9
Daley, Richard, 33,35
Dmochowski-Sanders, Henry, 4
Dmowski, Roman, 18,19
Douglas, Stephen, 5
Dyniewicz, Wladyslaw, 7
Dzierozynski, Francis, 3

Eisenhower, Dwight, 30,31

Feehan, Patrick A., 9
Fourier, Francois, 4
Funk, Casimir, 17

Gieryk, Theodore, 7
Giller, Agaton, 9
Gola, Thomas, 38
Greene, Nathaniel, 2
Gribbs, Roman, 37
Grochowski, Leon, 30,31,33,37
Gronouski, John, 33,34,37
Grotowski, Jerzy, 37
Gunther, Blair, 26
Gurowski, Adam, 5
Gzowski, Casimir, 7

Haiman, Miecislaus, 2,6,24,27
Halecki, Oscar, 26,27,29
Haller, Joseph, 19,20
Hodur, Francis, 11,15,29,30
Humphrey, Hubert, 36

Jastremski, Leon, 8
Jaworski, Leon, 38
Jefferson, Thomas, 2
Jerzmanowski, Erazmus, 10
Jogues, Isaac, 1
Justin, Father, 23

Kalussowski, Henry, 5
Karga, Joseph, 6,7
Kelly, Eric, 23
Kennedy, John F., 32,33
King, Martin Luther, 34
Kiolbassa, Peter, 6,7,10,11
Kleczka, John, 19,20
Kolbe, Maximilian, 39
Kolm, Richard, 40
Koprowski, Hilary, 38
Kosinski, Jerzy, 36
Kosciuszko, Tadeusz, 1,2,3,4,
  14,15,40
Kowal, Chester, 33
Kowalski, 10
Kozlowski, Anthony, 12,13,15
Krol, John Joseph, 33,35,40
Kruszka, Michael, 10
Kruszka, Waclaw, 13,14
Krzycki, Leo, 26,27
Krzyzanowski, Wlodzimierz,
  5,6
Kuniczak, W.S. (Jack), 35
Kunz, Stanley, 10

Landowska, Wanda, 25
Lange, Oscar, 27,28
Lincoln, Abraham, 5

MacCracken, Henry Noble, 22